T0041284

PRAISE FOR *DIG*

"*Digital MD* is a groundbreaking exploration of the technology-healthcare interface. Through a deep dive into the digital health ecosystem, this work provides a timely and comprehensive guide to the ever-evolving landscape of patient care. Dr. Kwo's commitment to fostering crosstalk between healthcare companies and technology pioneers makes this a must-read for professionals seeking to understand and impact the future of digital health innovation."

—Bob Langer, Institute Professor, MIT; Cofounder, Moderna

"Dr. Kwo's experience as a physician, digital entrepreneur, payer, and educator gives her a unique perspective on how US healthcare operates today. She has great insight on how we can transition to place all patients at the center of all that we do. In *Digital MD*, Liz discusses how big data and technology can support providers in delivering better patient care."

—Amy Mosser, President, HCPro; Former Interim CEO,
American Health Information Management Association

"There are eight billion people on earth and less than half have any kind of healthcare. The immense challenge for providers and payers is in expanding access, affordability, and accountability for all. We cannot train enough doctors nor build enough hospitals and clinics to solve these issues; the solutions will emerge from the nexus of technology and software. In this brilliant primer, Kwo clearly explains how digitalization in healthcare has evolved with advances in technology and most recently catalyzed by artificial intelligence. With her rich background in medicine, business, and investing, Dr. Kwo brings a unique and highly informed perspective on what is meant by 'Digital Medicine' and a promising and realistic view of the future of healthcare."

—**Stephen Oesterle, MD**, Former Sr. VP of
Medicine and Technology, Medtronic Plc.

"Dr. Kwo gives her optimistic and pragmatic take on the opportunity for incumbents and innovators to lock arms and figure out how to make our healthcare system more sustainable (and dare we say delightful!). She is a singular mind in the digital health space, and her words will inspire all who read this book."

—**Julie Yoo**, General Partner, a16z; Cofounder, Kyruus

Digital MD by Dr. Liz Kwo is a novel reference that delves into the transformative power of digital technology in the healthcare industry. Kwo's expertise and insights are evident throughout, making the book a must-read for anyone interested in how digital technology will impact the future of healthcare and how to play a role in the revolution."

—**Peter Barrett**, Partner, Atlas Venture; Executive
Fellow, Harvard Business School

"Dr. Kwo delves into the dynamic realm of evolving healthcare technology in today's medical practice with her book, *Digital MD*. It's the perfect guide for healthcare professionals seeking to integrate evolving technology into their practice, unlocking the potential of healthcare. This timely resource explores the seamless fusion of human minds with machines, making it the right book for the right time in advancing healthcare."

—**Rebecca Love**, CEO, Nurse Approved

"As a primary care doctor practicing for over twenty-five years, *Digital MD* resonates. It showcases the complexity of healthcare while providing a landscape analysis and road map for the coming wave of digital solutions that will break over fortress medicine. We need different, not better; because better than what exists is still awful."

—Jordan Shlain, Founder and CEO, Private Medical

"A terrific read that takes you behind the scenes and clearly shows how best to navigate the complexities of the healthcare system."

—Michael Greeley, Cofounder and General
Partner, Flare Capital Partners

"This book provides a balanced and informed perspective on the challenges and opportunities presented by digital health. Dr. Kwo's practical approach and real-world examples make this book an invaluable resource for healthcare leaders and entrepreneurs."

—Gaye L. Bok, Partner, AI and Digital Innovation Venture Fund, Mass General Brigham

"*Digital MD* is a well-researched and thoughtfully presented examination of how technology is reshaping the healthcare industry. This is a relevant book that explores the intersection of medicine and technology. Her writing is engaging, and her expertise in the field is evident throughout the book. *Digital MD* is a must-read for anyone curious about the future of healthcare. It's both informative and forward-thinking, providing valuable insights into the role of technology in improving patient care."

—Michael McCullough, MD, Founder and CEO, BrainMind;
Assistant Clinical Professor of Emergency Medicine, UCSF

"Unlike other books that veer too far into either utopian promises or dystopian warnings, *Digital MD* stands out for offering a balanced perspective. It ensures that readers come away with a comprehensive understanding of what digital healthcare really involves. Dr. Kwo is among the most insightful individuals I've had the pleasure of meeting. Whenever she shares her thoughts, it's always something you need to listen to, or in this case, read."

—Jared S. Taylor, Founder and CEO, Slice of Healthcare

"Liz Kwo's book, *Digital MD,* is a compelling and insightful guide to navigating the transformative landscape of digital healthcare in America. Kwo provides a comprehensive view of the '5P' stakeholders—pioneers, providers, patients, payers, and policymakers—embracing the promise of personalized, tech-enabled healthcare. Her book not only dispels industry myths and addresses challenges but also offers practical recommendations, making it an indispensable resource for both seasoned healthcare executives and tech pioneers looking to thrive in the evolving digital healthcare ecosystem."

—Gil Addo Jr., CEO and Cofounder, RubiconMD

Digital MD

Digital MD

REVOLUTIONIZING THE
FUTURE OF HEALTHCARE

Dr. Liz Kwo

Advantage | Books

Copyright © 2024 by Dr. Liz Kwo.

All rights reserved. No part of this book may be used or reproduced in any manner whatsoever without prior written consent of the author, except as provided by the United States of America copyright law.

Published by Advantage, Charleston, South Carolina.
Member of Advantage Media.

ADVANTAGE is a registered trademark, and the Advantage colophon is a trademark of Advantage Media Group, Inc.

Printed in the United States of America.

10 9 8 7 6 5 4 3 2 1

ISBN: 978-1-64225-801-1 (Paperback)
ISBN: 978-1-64225-800-4 (eBook)

Library of Congress Control Number: 2024905897

Cover design by David Taylor.
Layout design by Lance Buckley.

This publication is designed to provide accurate and authoritative information in regard to the subject matter covered. It is sold with the understanding that the publisher is not engaged in rendering legal, accounting, or other professional services. If legal advice or other expert assistance is required, the services of a competent professional person should be sought.

Advantage Media helps busy entrepreneurs, CEOs, and leaders write and publish a book to grow their business and become the authority in their field. Advantage authors comprise an exclusive community of industry professionals, idea-makers, and thought leaders. Do you have a book idea or manuscript for consideration? We would love to hear from you at **AdvantageMedia.com**.

To my family, the ones we are born into and the ones we choose.

In life's journey, paths may twist and bend,
yet in companionship, true joys ascend.

CONTENTS

ACKNOWLEDGMENTS

I want to acknowledge and thank my great mentors who ultimately gave me the impetus to write this book. As immigrants from Taiwan, my parents were the first of those mentors, and I've been learning ever since, inspired by their determination to provide for their family. Now I have a family of my own, and I yearn to see the future generation of leaders creating an upward trajectory in healthcare. In the same way I was mentored, I urge my mentees to prove their competence early on in professional interactions, and it's been an effective strategy—for them and for me and one mirrored by the purpose of this book—to inspire innovation.

As a female entrepreneur in health tech, I was advised to build a community and articulate my goals to people within the community very clearly. And that required being unabashed about inviting others to join me as costewards of a vision and journey to help transform healthcare. Acting on others' good advice has fueled my forward progress, both personally and professionally.

Working collaboratively with the stakeholders I call the 5Ps (providers, patients, payers, pioneers, policymakers), our healthcare ecosystem has a shared North Star. That North Star orientation defines success as the digitization of a transformed health system providing patients with better health outcomes, equity, and affordable care. I'm inviting every stakeholder to see how rigorous science and agile innovation can come together to reimagine the new global era of digital healthcare.

A real-world example of this new digital healthcare is the way Walmart in Mexico is meeting the country's huge need for affordable healthcare. For $1.50 (USD) monthly, the company launched a health membership that provides basic primary care to anyone who needs it. Customers gain access to a monthly medical consultation at the physicians' office located inside stores, 24/7 medical assistance by phone, and unlimited telemedicine access. Nutritionist and psychological support are also available through digital consultations, and members can buy discounted medications at the in-store pharmacy. This benefits millions of people who needed access to basic quality care. This is the future of healthcare.

> **Without the experiences and support from experts in the industry, this book would not exist. The world is better with those who create community and are willing to share their gift of time.**

In the vast expanse of the universe, I am grateful to call upon a community of experts, colleagues, and friends. While I cannot thank everyone who contributed in many ways to this book, I would like to give a special thanks to Katherine Sham and Zoe Bergin for their help researching and organizing this book. I would also like to acknowledge Kathryn Rowerdink, Beth McMahon, and Rachel Lissak who elevated this book with their wisdom and insights.

FOREWORD

The world of healthcare is undergoing a significant transformation, with technological advancements playing a crucial role in shaping the future of care delivery. Healthcare is still the most trusted profession on earth, with most people implicitly trusting their physician during the times they're most vulnerable. Yet, fewer people today have a primary care doctor to help at such times because of accessibility issues and staff shortages. Digital health tech is filling that care gap with the online provider access and the health apps now permeating the digital landscape. The COVID-19 pandemic taught even the tech resistant to order online and to expect an immediate response. Now both patients and consumers have learned how to access healthcare remotely, permanently fueling the trend toward digital health.

As the baby boomer population ages, it's putting pressure on healthcare systems globally. Today, this long-predicted "boomer bulge" is creating longer lines and tighter schedules for caregivers to manage. At the same time, Gens X and Z and millennials increasingly trust technology more than they trust their local hospital brand or even their doctor. That trend is being driven by the fact they have to wait months to see their caregiver. This cohort of patients is more empowered, changing the vernacular from "the doctor will see you now" to "the patient will schedule an appointment today." And they will rate, score, and comment publicly on their provider organizations based on their experiences.

With all that in mind, Dr. Kwo highlights the role of the advanced language models used in transformative technologies, such as ChatGPT. This artificial intelligence (AI)-powered conversational platform can converse with the average patient on virtually any clinical question. ChatGPT's ability to understand the nuances of human language and provide tailored responses makes it an invaluable tool in healthcare. Patients can interact with ChatGPT through their mobile phones, making it a convenient and accessible option for many. As the health industry continues to evolve, such digital health technologies will revolutionize healthcare and become increasingly important in delivering high-quality patient care.

The complexity of medical conditions and the need to treat the "total person"—including their health, habits, nutrition, and mental well-being—have made healthcare more challenging. At the same time, the principle of "do no harm" still holds, and patient safety remains a top priority. Precision medicine is one important innovation supporting that principle. Two decades of genetic sequencing has brought this diagnostic breakthrough to mainstream health protocols and into the digital shopping cart. With the combination of phenotypic diagnostics and now genotypic supplement, digital health has become a crucial pillar of modern medicine. By connecting patients to their DNA through genomics, precision medicine has improved patient outcomes in a way that's changed healthcare permanently. Future patient "trust" will likely be with those provider organizations who also have the patient's genome.

This book, *Digital MD: Revolutionizing the Future of Healthcare*, delves into these and other important topics and maps out the strategies needed to shape the future of healthcare delivery. Dr. Liz Kwo brilliantly examines the key trends and innovations in digital health, including precision medicine, patient safety, and the integration of AI and genomic medicine. She also provides insights and solutions for the challenges currently facing the healthcare industry and those it's likely to face in the future. In doing so, she offers her vision for creating the more efficient, effective patient-centric, digitally evolving healthcare system of the future.

—Paul M. Black, PB Global Ventures

PREFACE

Tech is making healthcare in America more affordable and accessible. Data and digital tools are aligning to become the cornerstone of healthcare's future—one that's personalized, predictive, preventive, prescriptive, and proactive. As a physician who is directly involved with this healthcare transformation, I can confirm the upheaval is happening quickly and spans the entire patient journey. Patients now have more options and mediums to access health services than ever before. And it's all thanks to the expanding array of technology being developed by health-tech pioneers working on the leading edge of digital innovation.

This digital-first, graduated approach to health services helps patients get their health questions answered more quickly and to connect with their providers more easily online—when, and how, they prefer. Like patients and providers, payers and policymakers also endorse the greater accessibility and efficiency of personalized, tech-enabled healthcare. The "5P" stakeholders, *pioneers, providers, patients, payers,* and *policymakers,* are embracing digital health tech's promise. They've seen the data and outcomes.

A DIGITAL-FIRST APPROACH

Providing this quality healthcare means giving patients the most appropriate, cost-effective medical and care services. Mindfully applying a digital-first approach is a win-win scenario for healthcare stakeholders and especially for payers—who are key. Payers are most critical to digital technology's implementation, availability, and sustainability because, in many cases, payers must be willing to fund specific healthcare tech before consumers can actually access it. This payer piece of the puzzle is of particular interest to me as I work to bring digital tech mainstream so that all stakeholders can benefit. Government laws and regulations that foster faster digital care adoption are necessary too—accelerated by the pandemic.

As I continue to operate in healthcare companies and serve as a director on boards, I know healthcare executives and tech pioneers are keenly aware of digital tech's benefits. Like me, they know those benefits are transforming the practice of medicine and care delivery. What's often misunderstood, however, is the way that tech gets adopted and paid for and how healthcare's 5P stakeholders are interacting as digital healthcare evolves. All of them are playing a pivotal role in the digital transformation of healthcare, and every one of these stakeholders has a lot to gain (and lose) in the ongoing disruption of the healthcare industry. To optimize their gain, I'm using the twenty-twenty vision of my professional hindsight to share the knowledge I've acquired as a digital health entrepreneur and payer executive within the industry.

THE LEARNING CURVE

Getting to this point of influence has required balancing my business performance with personal goals. It's facilitated a more holistic approach to achievement as I've had to learn how to maintain the work-self balance that's been so essential to my continued, long-term success. While trying to start a family in 2013, for example, I was recruited to become vice president of provider networks at American Well, a company innovating in telemedicine. It was thrilling to set up one of the nation's first online-provider groups, connecting to patients via video. However, I had a stillbirth in 2013 and, afterward, began channeling my energy instead into founding a company to support patients looking for virtual second opinions.

I founded InfiniteMD with two brilliant friends. As CEO, I built a tech-enabled global service platform where patients could receive expert medical advice both synchronously and asynchronously. My cofounders and I sold InfiniteMD in 2020 after I joined Elevance and became their deputy chief clinical officer, tasked with building clinical and digital innovation tools.

Still, I wish I'd known just how much the industry landscape can shift whenever there's a political "changing of the guards" from one administration or leader to another. I learned that's when new healthcare agendas are set that can expand or constrict a company's options. And I wish I'd understood the complex US payer *ecosystem* before I started my digital health companies and had to parse how payers think, make decisions, sell, make a profit, and build partnerships.

The Healthcare Ecosystem

I mention the payer ecosystem because payer priorities are one of the primary forces driving digital transformation in the healthcare *ecosystem*. There's that word again: *ecosystem*. It's an apt descriptor of healthcare's interconnected and competing interests. Knowing how those stakeholders interact and which factors are impacting and motivating (or constraining) them is essential. In a business context, healthcare's stakeholders are motivated by the positive economic and financial returns.

The way these systems function involves three competing, but integral, elements you can think of as the points of a triangle: *access*, *quality*, and *cost containment*. Maintaining equal balance between all three elements is challenging but necessary and doable. Optimizing these elements results in better profitability and functionality for every stakeholder. That's especially true for payers.

This book will explain these aspects of the payer ecosystem and more so that you can better understand how to navigate healthcare's multifaceted, growing, and increasingly digital landscape. Opting in sooner, rather than later, to that landscape is a smart business move, so I'm sharing key takeaways from my experiences. I want tech pioneers and those starting out in healthcare to benefit from what I've discovered about the inner workings of the healthcare industry. I'll dispel prevalent industry myths and provide an inside look at how digital healthcare technology is financed. This book is written to help you extract business insights across the digital health spectrum; it is not meant to be all-encompassing across payer contracts or provider relationships or every type of technology. My purpose in writing the book is to construct a bridge linking corporations and digital tech pioneers so that they can work together to build quality healthcare products and solutions for patients and care providers. Ultimately, we can, as a society, create better, more sustainable healthcare options that will benefit patients now and into the future.

INVESTING IN DIGITAL HEALTH

Whatever your 5P stakeholder role, you'll need to know something about the biggest opportunities and obstacles for innovation. I'll analyze relevant interactions between the 5P stakeholders and those considered secondary (regulators, researchers, application developers, medical device manufacturers, employers, and distributors) to showcase where openness for innovation is likely to be found.

I'll not only address specific challenges but also identify the concepts, tasks, and skills professionals need to master in order to adopt and implement the appropriate innovations. For those of you who are tech pioneers, I'll also recommend goals for going digital with your healthcare services. And I'll cover several aspects of healthcare operations, including new technologies, mobile health (mHealth), best practices, and quality improvement, as well as privacy, security, and ethics issues.

In the following chapters, I'll provide detailed examples of corporate thought leaders who've implemented digital healthcare successfully and what that means for their digital products/solutions companies. You'll see how these health leaders involved with diagnostics, devices, therapeutics, and care delivery (both episodic and chronic) have positioned themselves on the leading edge of the digital healthcare transformation.

To make such information practical and applicable, I'll share the stories of some of these corporate leaders explaining how they select and implement digital health technologies, including:

- how a hospital CEO can benefit from AI-enhanced telehealth services that increase patient satisfaction and outcomes while maximizing existing resources,
- the reason a healthcare insurance company's chief health officer would consider paying for liquid biopsy and cell therapy,
- why a nursing home CEO would want to implement remote patient monitoring (RPM) and a description of existing options to pay for it,

- an employer benefits manager's logic for deciding it's efficient to pay for maternity or musculoskeletal digital health apps as part of their benefit offering to employees, and

- why the CTO of an insurance company would be wise to pay for data analytics that track nonmedical factors influencing health outcomes.

A more global perspective is essential too, so I'll share the major factors at play as digital health tech disrupts the larger healthcare industry. If you're a decision-maker or influencer at your organization, this information will help you stay abreast of broad developments and provide a road map of a tech-adoption process you can follow. And if you're a pioneer trying to grow and scale your business, I'll show you how corporate and governmental healthcare entities analyze and value innovation so that you, too, can be better equipped to work strategically within that payer ecosystem. Whether you're a C-suite executive or a tech pioneer responsible for developing new digital health technology, I'll provide the global view of the digital healthcare transformation you're going to need to make smart business decisions.

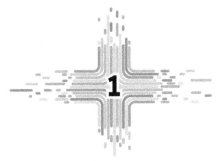

DIGITAL PILLS
FOR EVERY ILL

How Digital Health Tech Will
Revolutionize Disease Management

Is the US healthcare system expensive, complicated, dysfunctional, or broken? The simple answer is yes to all.

—ROBERT H. SHMERLING, MD, HARVARD MEDICAL SCHOOL

Every ambitious entrepreneur needs great problems to solve. In my case, that's meant introducing innovations to help the ailing US healthcare system. Although it has many strengths, including world-renowned hospitals and medical professionals, the overall status of the system indicates deeply rooted issues. After "checking the vitals" of American healthcare, I would even go so far as to say it requires lifesaving treatment. Its symptoms, like the millions of people it strives to serve, are chronic in nature and in desperate need of corrective intervention. Fortunately, the US has a robust research and development infrastructure that's created advanced medical technology to provide that intervention.

So what are the pressing US healthcare "symptoms" pioneers need to know about? For starters, America experiences the *worst* health outcomes when compared to thirty-eight similarly wealthy nations in the Organisation for Economic Co-operation and Development (OECD).[1] As of 2021, that meant those living in America died younger and were less healthy—despite the fact that the US spent the most on healthcare per person and as a share of gross domestic product (GDP). Back then, the US was already spending nearly 18 percent of its GDP on healthcare, yet Americans still had the *lowest life expectancy* at birth, highest death rates for avoidable or treatable conditions, and most maternal and infant mortality and was one of the OECD countries with the greatest incidence of suicide.[2]

To top it all off, the US has the highest incidence of people with multiple chronic conditions and an obesity rate nearly twice that of the OECD average.[3] Some of these negative outcomes can be traced to inequity in care delivery, lack of universal health coverage, and an emphasis on treatment instead of prevention. When combined with a litigious medical malpractice environment, all of these factors interact to diminish the efficiency and effectiveness of patient care.

DOCTOR, WE HAVE A PROBLEM

Many of the US health system's failings stem from its fragmented design. Its structural complexity is such a huge problem that I could write an in-depth book on the serious issues that causes. But *this* book is about how digital technologies can solve many of healthcare's existing shortcomings within the structure that already exists. Regarding those lacks, I would make the argument that most of the

---

1   Munira Z. Gunja, Evan D. Gumas, Reginald D. Williams II, "US Health Care from a Global Perspective, 2022: Accelerating Spending, Worsening Outcomes?" Commonwealth Fund, January 2020, https://www.commonwealthfund.org/publications/issue-briefs/2023/jan/us-health-care-global-perspective-2022.

2   Ibid.

3   Ibid.

health system's challenges can be linked to a singular reason: US healthcare wasn't designed to combat or manage chronic diseases at the epidemic levels occurring now.

When the US health system was originally designed in the 1950s after World War II, its purpose was to treat acute care ailments. Healthcare was meant to be allocated for episodic, acute treatment at a time healthcare costs were still relatively low. But that's changed, and now chronic disease has become so prevalent that the US system needs to redesign and shift the fundamentals of how care is organized and delivered.

What are the differences between an acute care–focused system and a chronic-focused system? An *acute care system* focuses on providing immediate and intensive care, whereas a *chronic-focused system* recognizes the need for ongoing medical monitoring, treatment, and support. This requires changes across the system in how care is delivered by shifting away from a more episodic and reactive model to a more proactive and preventive one: one that digital tools can deliver, as we'll discuss later.

The shift isn't proving to be an easy one. Everything from how health information systems are utilized and implemented to how the system's payment and financing structure incentivizes care are having to be realigned. Looking at healthcare financing models, for example, we're trying to move from an acute care system with a fee-for-service payment model to a more chronic-focused model that incentivizes outcomes and care coordination.

In the context of that new model, incentivizing prevention makes sense. I say that because some chronic ailments are preventable. So why aren't individuals putting their health first in their lifestyle choices? Some in healthcare reason that people living with chronic diseases could "make better choices," but system infrastructure and socioeconomic circumstances make this difficult. Since over 50 percent of Americans suffer from a chronic disease,[4] it does warrant taking a step back and looking at the systemic causes creating poor lifestyles in our society.

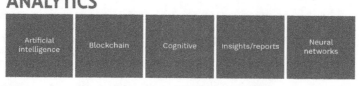

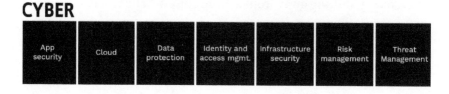

Driving Progress: How companies view their ecosystem from the leadership point of view.

Other parts of the world are already doing that. In Europe, for example, some countries have instituted regulations that support good nutrition and healthy eating habits. But similar initiatives haven't always received support from US voters. Those initiatives include

---

4   Bill Siwicki, "How Remote Patient Monitoring Improves Care & Saves Money for Chronic Care," Healthcare IT News, June 28, 2022, accessed January 2023, https://www.healthcareitnews.com/news/how-remote-patient-monitoring-improves-care-saves-money-chronic-care.

front-of-pack nutrition labeling, restrictions on marketing to children, school food standards, sugar taxes, and trans-fat restrictions. Why aren't Americans supporting internationally proven and tested government interventions for food that will combat the chronic disease epidemic? That's a really good question.

One theory is that some policies reveal our health system as a private system, and, therefore, another person's lifestyle choices are their right. Not all Americans hold the same views on nutrition regulations, and opinions and attitudes on lifestyle vary. However, poor health outcomes have significant cost implications for the entire system, and the largest burden of total health spending is borne by the US federal government and American taxpayers.[5]

The individualistic approach to healthcare in our country is reflected by our lack of universal health coverage and the absence of public health prevention policies as compared to many OECD countries. This failing is made painfully clear by the fact that the typical American lives in a town without sidewalks and with limited access to adequate, affordable, and nutritious foods.[6] It's clear that change is desperately needed. The reality of the current chronic disease crisis shows the public needs to support health initiatives and that the health system itself need to change. At this point, I'm sure you get the picture.

---

5   "National Health Expenditure Fact Sheet," Centers for Medicare and Medicaid Services, accessed January 2023, https://www.cms.gov/research-statistics-data-and-systems/statistics-trends-and-reports/nationalhealthexpenddata/nhe-fact-sheet.

6   Robert Steuteville, "Walkable Places Gain Market Share, Economic Impact," Public Square (blog), Congress for New Urbanism, February 2, 2023, https://www.cnu.org/publicsquare/2023/02/02/demise-walkable-places-greatly-exaggerated; "Poor Nutrition," Centers for Disease Control and Prevention, accessed January 2023, https://www.cdc.gov/chronicdisease/resources/publications/factsheets/nutrition.htm.

TOO BIG TO FIX?

After reading through the preceding list of issues affecting our care system, it's clear we need to prescribe the appropriate solutions to restore the *healthy* in healthcare. As a provider, former payer, and digital health-tech pioneer, I'm cognizant of the magnitude of the problems. I'm sure you are too. *It's too hard to fix,* you might be thinking. But that's not the case. And you'll understand why once you grasp the approach stakeholders have already started using to cure the underlying problems.

A new kind of prevention-based healthcare is desperately needed. Faced with the magnitude of this epidemic, you might question whether chronic diseases can actually be addressed through preventive care. The answer is yes! More than 90 percent of type 2 diabetes, 80 percent of coronary artery diseases (CAD), 70 percent of strokes, and 70 percent of colon cancers can be ameliorated (meaning, they are *preventable*) by a combination of lifestyle choices, including avoiding smoking, obesity, and overuse of alcohol, while proactively ensuring moderate physical activity and good nutrition.[7] Sleep is a key health behavior too, since sleeping less than seven hours per day is associated with an increased risk of developing chronic conditions, such as obesity, diabetes, and high blood pressure.[8]

So how does understanding this system and the current chronic disease crisis impact health-tech pioneers? It would be overly simplistic to say that digital health tools will solve everything. But I've seen how incredible challenges can drive the acceptance and utilization of incredible innovation, and the epidemic of chronic disease is proving

---

7   "Disease Control Priorities in Developing Countries," National Center for Biotechnology Information, accessed January 2023, https://www.ncbi.nlm.nih.gov/books/NBK11795.

8   "1 in 3 Adults Don't Get Enough Sleep," Centers for Disease Control and Prevention, February 18, 2016, https://archive.cdc.gov/#/details?url=https://www.cdc.gov/media/releases/2016/p0215-enough-sleep.html.

to be one such challenge. Implementing the efficiencies of digital health-tech solutions is especially important in light of the fact that the American population is aging, and healthcare costs will continue to rise rapidly. As you might expect, the elderly (ages eighty-five and older) require the most health services per capita, and that segment of the population is on a sharp upward trajectory from five million in 2005 to a projected nine million in 2030.[9]

If no change occurs to inculcate preventive measures and practices into healthcare, the existing strain on the healthcare system will cost *everyone* dearly. By 2027, the Centers for Medicare and Medicaid Services (CMS) projects the government (federal, state, and local) will finance 47 percent of national health spending at a cost of $6 trillion, consuming 19.4 percent of the country's GDP.[10] Waiting for an aging population to develop chronic disease and then treating/managing their chronic disease symptoms for the rest of their lives is *not* a viable solution—either for the country as a whole or for elders' quality of life. The result of sticking with the status quo is inevitable failure of the goal of healthcare that is promoting good health. An apt analogy for the current health system is trying to bail water out of a sinking boat. *Fixing* the boat, that is, healthcare, is the only solution. As medical costs continue to grow, the negative impact on stakeholders in the health industry will continue to grow too.[11] This is creating an urgent, pervasive need for entrepreneurs to help reduce healthcare's inefficiencies so that providers can continue to offer quality care.

---

9   "Retooling for an Aging America: Building the Health Care Workforce," National Center for Biotechnology Information, accessed January 2023, https://www.ncbi.nlm.nih.gov/books/NBK215400/.

10   "CMS Office of the Actuary Releases 2018-2027 Projections of National Health Expenditures," CMS.gov, February 20, 2019, https://www.cms.gov/newsroom/press-releases/cms-office-actuary-releases-2018-2027-projections-national-health-expenditures.

11   "2019 Behind the Numbers," PwC Health Research Institute, accessed January 2023, https://www.pwc.com/us/en/health-industries/health-research-institute/assets/pdf/hri-behind-the-numbers-2019.pdf.

WHOSE DECISION IS IT ANYWAY?

Having documented healthcare's problems and highlighted the urgent need for change, I have to ask a crucial question. *Do Americans really want to fix the healthcare industry? And do American physicians actually want to use health tech?* Providers like myself are advocating for its use. But what about patients? Are they open to the diagnostic and treatment benefits digital health offers? The answer is *yes!*

Patients are already looking for a more consumer-centric kind of experience. Patients are often the end consumer of health-tech innovations and the ones most motivated to access new healthcare products and services. Even so, it's worth noting that the end user is not always the decision-maker in our health system, nor is the payer. This presents the question, Who is the health-tech pioneer's true customer? The answer informs the commercial model.

I'll answer that question by providing a helpful analogy. Consider a product like children's toys—the end user is the child, but the decision-maker and the payer is the parent. In this scenario, the toy designer needs to consider both the interest of the child and the interest of the parents. The child might want a toy that's filled with candy and plays their favorite song loudly on repeat. The parent, however, is thinking about the educational impact of the toy, the price point, and the ability for their kid to play quietly. In the end, the parent is paying for the toy, and the toy maker may need to prioritize the buyer.

How does this relate to the adoption of health-tech innovation? It's a simple analogy for the plight of the health-tech pioneer in a third-party payer health system, where the third-party payer might be employers, health insurance companies, or government programs, such as Medicaid and Medicare. Although many payer and patient interests are aligned, such as wanting quality care, the interests of those two stakeholders don't always align.

In the case of self-insured employers, they may choose products that retain their employees and enhance productivity. In contrast, with fully insured coverage where insurers design the benefit fit, they may aim to provide services that keep medical costs low and review a return on the investment for twelve months. Suffice it to say that the disparity between different stakeholders' agendas makes the health industry complicated.

So it's important to think about the decision-making processes and the incentives for all parties involved. Fortunately, there are segments of the industry that can benefit from a direct-to-consumer commercial model where the patient is both the buyer and the end user. This offers the patient more choices in their fight against chronic disease. That's the case when patients purchase and use devices like fitness trackers and sleep monitors as part of their preventive health measures, which is now becoming more widely covered by self-insured employers.

CONSUMERS WANT ACCESS TO HEALTH TECH

Whether in a direct-to-consumer market or a third-party-payer model that has more autonomy, the end user is still the patient, so all other stakeholders should focus on serving patients' health needs first and foremost. As I previously noted, patients are also consumers who want access to health tech, and a growing number of those consumers have come to rely on the practical help provided by fitness trackers, sleep monitors, and wearables that detect arrhythmias. Since consumers prioritize wellness, it's a unique opportunity for the payer (and employer), provider, and pioneer stakeholders to prioritize and meet that need.

WHY START A DIGITAL HEALTH COMPANY

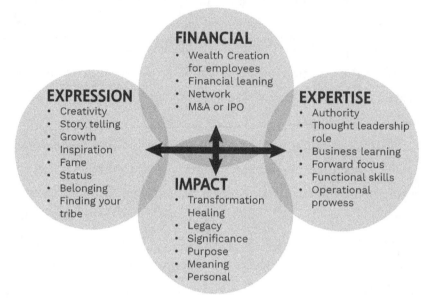

Why Start a Digital Health Company? Founders of digital health companies develop healthcare products and services to fill gaps in the existing healthcare system.

The bottom line is that health consumers want what's available in other industry sectors: being able to choose options and readily see the price and quality of those options. For consumer-facing digital health tech, that quality assurance is usually provided by the Food and Drug Administration (FDA). But the massive wave of health-tech innovation currently underway is making it difficult for the federal agency to keep up with the deluge of direct-to-consumer technologies currently inundating the market. One reason is that digital health tech is constantly pushing the leading edge as an increasing number of those technologies are targeting more complex health issues. As a stopgap measure, the FDA is regulating the quality and safety of digital health with multiple new committees and programs offering pre-approval for software and medical devices from companies meeting the FDA's standards of excellence in quality and safety.

At the same time, the expense of conventionally provided care is accelerating consumers' motivation to find health-tech alternatives that can help them manage their health needs more effectively and affordably. As costs rise, a growing number of Americans are bypassing traditional routes of care altogether because they simply can't afford it. An estimated 112 million (44 percent) adults in the US struggle to pay for healthcare, and over double that number (93 percent) don't think what they pay is worth the cost.[12] This is why getting digital health tech into the hands of consumers struggling to afford more conventional solutions should be a high priority for policymakers, payers, and providers.

During the ongoing chronic disease epidemic, it's sobering that adults in better health are the ones more likely to seek medical care compared to those in the worst health who report delaying, or not getting, medical care because of cost.[13] Making health technology options available to this underserved patient group is a critically important way to provide them with better access to health services.

In addition to the patient benefits of digital health tech, provider and payer stakeholders can benefit from digital healthcare's three-pronged, *simultaneous* solution for the current healthcare crisis:

---

12   "112 Million Americans Struggle to Afford Healthcare," West Health, March 20, 2023, https://www.westhealth.org/press-release/112-million-americans-struggle-to-afford-healthcare/.

13   Shameek Rakshit, Krutika Amin, and Cynthia Cox, "How Does Cost Affect Access to Care?" Peterson-KFF Health System Tracker, May 22, 2020, https://www.healthsystemtracker.org/chart-collection/cost-affect-access-care/.

1. *Manages existing chronic disease more effectively, efficiently, and affordably*
2. *Prevents chronic disease from developing in the first place*
3. *Measures outcomes with digital data to prove efficacy and patient benefit*

As the US healthcare system becomes increasingly dysfunctional, leveraging the benefits of this threefold solution is crucial.[14] Using more efficient, cost-effective management of chronic diseases and a gradual transition to incentivizing and facilitating chronic disease prevention is the only logical course of action.

MEASURABLE OUTCOMES IMPROVE HEALTHCARE

Fortunately, federal policymakers and other stakeholders understand the transformative importance of digital health tech. In fact, CMS is actively promoting the use of digital tech through their Council for Technology & Innovation as well as their Digital Service. One reason for their endorsement is that digital health technology supports the federal agency's expanding value-based care (VBC) initiative to improve healthcare. VBC focuses on quality of care, provider performance, and the patient experience.[15] This plays into that shift we were discussing earlier in this chapter—the one moving healthcare from a focus on acute care to one addressing the care and prevention of chronic diseases.

---

14   Robert H. Shmerling, "Is Our Healthcare System Broken?" Harvard Health Publishing, July 13, 2021, https://www.health.harvard.edu/blog/is-our-healthcare-system-broken-202107132542.

15   "Value-Based Care," CMS.gov, accessed March 21, 2024, https://www.cms.gov/priorities/innovation/key-concepts/value-based-care.

In light of this shift in healthcare's focus, VBC goals are challenging all healthcare providers to achieve three objectives:

1. *Improve the quality of patient care*
2. *Create better patient outcomes*
3. *Reduce the cost of care*

Multiple alternative payment models exist to tackle these goals for VBC, including pay-for-performance, shared savings and shared risk models, and bonus payments for achieving specific goals. It's important for pioneers to understand the structure of new payment models to ensure that their product has a sustainable commercial strategy.

These new financing models have created a shift in how healthcare funding is spent, and that change has created opportunities for new players and entrepreneurship. In 2021 alone, groups of doctors, hospitals, and other providers in Accountable Care Organizations (ACOs) saved Medicare $1.6 billion overall by offering coordinated VBC to Medicare patients.[16] And ACOs are just one of the three main VBC reimbursement models. The others include Integrated Healthcare Networks (IHNs) and the Medicare Shared Savings Plan (MSSP). In the case of a Cigna IHN, for example, employers saved more than $1,400 per member (annually) on employees enrolled in a Cigna IHN that coordinated medical, pharmacy, and behavioral benefits.[17] And MSSPs saved more than $1.6 billion in 2021 while

---

16   "Medicare Shared Savings Program Saves Medicare More than $1.6 billion in 2021 and Continues to Deliver High Quality Care," Centers for Medicare and Medicaid Services, August 30, 2022, https://www.cms.gov/newsroom/press-releases/medicare-shared-savings-program-saves-medicare-more-16-billion-2021-and-continues-deliver-high.

17   Victoria Bailey, "Cigna's Integrated Health Plan Reduced Care Costs for Employers," Healthcare IT News, August 11, 2022, https://healthpayerintelligence.com/news/cignas-integrated-health-plan-reduced-care-costs-for-employers.

delivering high-quality care.[18] Since CMS is the biggest payer, all three of those CMS reimbursement arrangements are continuing to reform US healthcare in a big way.

By corralling public and private health services into a less fragmented, more streamlined healthcare system, all stakeholders stand to benefit. That trend will also continue to speed up the implementation of digital health throughout the healthcare system. In fact, digital technology has now been developed and applied to every aspect of health and healthcare.[19] Companies that move to provide that technology to consumers stand to win over slower competitors.

THE DIRECT-TO-CONSUMER SPACE

The health-sector companies giving consumers access to digital health tech in the form of tests, devices, and services aren't doing that through a health provider or medical facility. So they don't participate in the three CMS payer reimbursement options I described earlier. But digital health-tech companies are still contributing to an overall reduction in US healthcare costs. Although consumers don't need a provider's prescription to access many at-home health devices and tests, they often partner with their doctors to understand the full use and benefit of their consumer health tech. So the use of consumer health tech isn't meant to replace or bypass providers. Rather, it's meant to fill a gap in existing care options and lower costs to the healthcare system. Buying directly from consumer health-tech companies is just

---

18 "Medicare Shared Savings Program Saves Medicare More than $1.6 billion in 2021 and Continues to Deliver High-Quality Care," U.S. Department of Health and Human Services, August 30, 2022, https://www.hhs.gov/about/news/2022/08/30/medicare-shared-savings-program-saves-medicare-more-than-1-6-billion-in-2021-and-continues-to-deliver-high-quality-care.html.

19 Amy Abernethy et al., "The Promise of Digital Health: Then, Now, and the Future," National Center for Biotechnology Information, September 9, 2022, https://www.ncbi.nlm.nih.gov/pmc/articles/PMC9499383/.

one reason for those savings since it usually means the cost billed to CMS or private insurance payers is lower.

Here's one example; while a single pair of non-sterile surgical gloves can cost as little as $1 when bought online, a hospital may charge a much higher price—let's say $53 per non-sterile pair (sterile are higher) in order to recoup the cost through medical claims. There are a myriad of other such medical items and services showing a dramatic billed-expense differential. In the case of medical tests, for example, the cost differential is often *much* higher. It's easy to understand how quickly inflated costs might add up. And it's the reason medical bills in the US are the most common reason for personal bankruptcy.[20] Medical bankruptcy statistics suggest that 17 percent of adults with healthcare debt had to declare bankruptcy or lose their home because of such debt as of 2022.[21] Unfortunately, over one million people, or 40 percent of Americans, are carrying medical debt.[22]

In the past, medical service and supply charges were somewhat arbitrary before the federal government started reforming the healthcare system with their VBC initiative. And it's good they did. Should a metabolic blood panel test cost $11 or $952? Patients have been charged both, but they won't know it before the test is administered. That's because patients don't usually know how much medical facilities will charge for individual tests or services like the aforementioned blood test. Yet, it's one of the most common tests in medicine, performed millions of times a year around the country.

---

20   "49+ Medical Bankruptcy Statistics for 2023," RetireGuide.com, accessed January 2023, https://www.retireguide.com/retirement-planning/risks/medical-bankruptcy-statistics/.

21   Ibid.

22   Anna Werner, "Investigation Finds 40% of all Adults in U.S. Struggle with Health Care Debt," CBSNews.com, June 17, 2022, https://www.cbsnews.com/news/health-care-debt-40-percent-us-adults/.

Why do hospitals charge such varied prices? This can be attributed to several factors, including hospitals using a cost-shifting approach to offset the expense of uncompensated care, high operating costs, lack of price transparency, and a fragmented payer system. But the varied pricing is also attributable to the market power and negotiating leverage that some health systems have with payers, especially in areas with low competition.

Because of the extreme pricing differences assigned to medical goods and services, price *visibility* is a top issue for all healthcare stakeholders. For patients, it means actually knowing the cost of tests and health tech up front. And as you might imagine, it's a welcome change. Everlywell is a direct-to-consumer testing company that transparently charges a price for testing, and purchasers can use flexible spending account (FSA)/health savings account (HSA) funds for payment.[23]

Consumers are catching on, especially since many have to carry high annual insurance deductibles to afford health insurance at all. If they're going to have to pay thousands of dollars out of pocket anyway, paying a lot less for the same test is a win for patients and consumers. This reality has become increasingly relevant since CMS started calling for price transparency. Those federal requirements went into effect in 2021, requiring hospitals to post a machine-readable list of their services and prices along with a patient-friendly tool to help shop for three hundred common services.

CMS leaders say the agency has handed out nearly five hundred warnings to hospitals who haven't met CMS's price transparency guidelines and now plans to streamline enforcement and standardize hospital reporting requirements.[24] When six hundred randomly sampled

---

23 "Best At-Home Metabolism Tests," Verywell Health, July 29, 2022, https://www. verywellhealth.com/best-at-home-metabolism-tests-5212225.

24 Dave Muoio, "CMS: Tighter Price Transparency Enforcement, Standardized Requirements for Hospitals Are on the Horizon," Fierce Healthcare, January 17, 2023, https://

hospitals were analyzed almost a year later, it found 82 percent had complied by providing consumer-friendly, searchable displays.[25] CMS encouraged pricing disclosure by increasing the penalty for noncompliance from over $100,000 annually per hospital to more than $2 million annually per hospital. Enforcement of the transparency requirements has also included more than 230 requests for corrective action plans for several medical facilities and organizations that hadn't complied.[26]

From a business perspective, making pricing visible to consumers is inevitably going to spur competition for patients who want to curb their medical costs. You get the picture: one that puts a growing cadre of savvy, proactive, cost-conscious consumers into the very middle of the healthcare ecosystem. Like CMS and other federal stakeholders, consumers/patients want to know their options and the *quality* of their options.

QUALITY ASSURANCE FOR HEALTH TECH

CMS is working hard to measure how well public and private health institutions and providers are meeting its goals of better patient care and outcomes for lower cost. To assess that, CMS and private health-sector payers rely on quality metrics provided by a nongovernment organization—the National Committee for Quality Assurance (NCQA). It's a useful partnership since the NCQA's Healthcare Effectiveness Data and Information Set (HEDIS) measures how well health-sector organizations, payers, and providers are meeting healthcare goals aligned to VBC.

---

www.fiercehealthcare.com/providers/cms-tighter-price-transparency-enforcement-standardized-requirements-are-horizon.

25   Ibid.

26   Ibid.

CMS instituted VBC back in 2005 to reorient the entire health system toward *quality versus quantity* for the sake of efficiency and effectiveness. Documenting results with HEDIS is a big part of CMS's efforts to streamline healthcare by indicating which aspects of healthcare work well and which don't.

Digital health tech is doing the same by providing a wealth of data that advances CMS's mission to promote health equity, expand coverage, and improve health outcomes. And the FDA is doing its part too by regulating the sale of medical device products and new home diagnostic tests that further patient-centric care and outcomes. FDA approval provides consumers with the means to assess the quality of the direct-to-consumer products they're offered online. That's crucial since consumers need to know the tests, tech, and services they're buying directly from companies are of good quality.

All healthcare stakeholders stand to benefit from VBC goals and health product assessments whether or not an organization, provider, or company has formally joined the VBC initiative. As a CMS initiative, VBC endorses the more preventive approach to healthcare that reduces costs while promoting better patient outcomes. Corporate payers and CMS are well aware of the cost differential between treating chronic disease "after the fact" and working to block it in the first place. That's why CMS has officially mandated the use of digital health tech, which can streamline, improve, and document better healthcare outcomes for patients. Digital tech has made it much easier to keep evidence of such outcomes with data proving results.

The Definition of "Value"

Since value-based healthcare doesn't define "value" per se, different stakeholders are able to use a multidimensional approach that considers a variety of metrics:

- *Clinical value:* better care coordination or a reduction in medical errors
- *Humanistic value:* improvements in patient experience, satisfaction, and quality of life
- *Economic value:* reduced out-of-pocket costs from efficient treatment or preventive care that eliminates the need for treatment altogether
- *Social value:* greater health equity

For providers, VBC means finding ways to prove or document the value of their health services to patients. Collecting accurate data is likely the biggest challenge in VBC, and it's even more challenging when multiple providers are utilizing different platforms. Using digital health tech in the form of electronic health records (EHRs) has proven to be the best way for healthcare professionals to gather reliable data.

It will also be easier for providers to get reimbursed for using health tech, as in the case of the Everlywell at-home colon cancer–screening test for adults over the age of forty-five: a type of testing that's received FDA and CMS support. As an example of the potential savings available to the healthcare system, the results of using the test are impressive. The average cost of a traditional colonoscopy in the US is $2,750 (though prices can range from $1,250 to $4,800). Since the out-of-pocket cost is only around $45, the savings to insurance payers is substantial, considering it's estimated that 16.6 million colonoscopies were performed in the US in 2019.[27] A rough calculation of the savings generated from this one procedure would be about $32 billion annually. That statistic doesn't even take into account the compliance rate for the traditional, invasive colonoscopy procedure that will undoubtedly be lower than for a noninvasive test, such as the one from Everlywell. This one example provides a glimpse of digital health tech's benefits to all stakeholders.

Although gastroenterologists may assume they'll suffer financial loss from performing fewer traditional colonoscopies, they can still benefit, as positive at-home tests require a traditional follow-up colonoscopy. Rather than viewing such changes as a threat to their status quo, busy providers can achieve the better demonstrated outcomes prioritized and rewarded by VBC models while also spending less time, expense, and effort. It's a win-win situation for all of healthcare's 5P stakeholders.

Whenever a new digital health technology comes on the scene, the 5P stakeholders will all look at the innovation through the lens of their own priorities. In the case of noninvasive tests for colon cancer, those who generate revenue from traditional colonoscopy procedures, such as gastroenterologists and hospitals, might tend to resist as I just discussed. Those who insist on doing so would be wise to rethink their position. Let me explain why; the vast majority of patients getting colonoscopies in the US will be participating in CMS-provided Medicare. And since CMS is currently facilitating the implementation of VBC, they will increasingly favor a home colon cancer screening (most cost-effective and efficient). Keep in mind that CMS expects all Medicare payments to go through value-based models by 2030.

---

27   "An Astounding 16.6 Million Colonoscopies Are Performed Annually in the United States," iData Research, September 12, 2022, https://idataresearch.com/an-astounding-19-million-colonoscopies-are-performed-annually-in-the-united-states/.

And providers and private insurers can expect policymakers to exert increasing financial pressure and incentives to push them in the same direction. In other words, sticking to the status quo isn't a sustainable option for most stakeholders.

MY EXECUTIVE TAKEAWAY

In the midst of the ongoing digital health-tech transformation, it's encouraging that CMS is using its significant clout as a federal policymaker and the largest health insurance payer in America to facilitate the use of digital health tech. The federal agency is covering more than 170 million people (in 2022) through Medicare, Medicaid, the Children's Health Insurance Program, and the Health Insurance Marketplace.[28] Since CMS is the health system's biggest payer stakeholder, it's proving to be a huge asset fostering the implementation of digital health tech among all of healthcare's 5P stakeholders.

> When it comes to the rise of digital health tech, patients and consumers are the ultimate winners and stand to benefit the most.

> A variety of amazing innovations are enabling patients to live a better quality of life instead of one marked by chronic disease.

> The 5P stakeholders are *patients, providers, payers, policymakers*, and *pioneers.*

> The 5Ps to scale digital health are *preventive, predictive, prescriptive, proactive*, and *personalized.*

> The three VBC reimbursement models include ACOs, IHNs, and MSSP.

---

28 "CMS Financial Report Fiscal Year 2022," Centers for Medicare and Medicaid Services, November 10, 2022, https://www.cms.gov/files/document/cms-financial-report-fiscal-year-2022.pdf.

The separate interests of healthcare's other stakeholders will be better served too, as digital health tech's efficiencies lower healthcare costs. That's critically important as those expenses grow. In 2023, federal subsidies for health insurance were estimated to be $1.8 trillion, or 7.0 percent of GDP. Those net subsidies are projected to reach $3.3 trillion, or 8.3 percent of GDP, in 2033.[29] In the chapter ahead, I want to share my insights about the business side of digital health-tech innovation. Let's take a look at that now.

---

29 "Federal Subsidies for Health Insurance Coverage for People under Age 65: 2023 to 2033," Congressional Budget Office, September 28, 2023, https://www.cbo.gov/publication/59273.

TWO SIDES OF THE SAME COIN

How Healthcare's Stakeholders Can Innovate to Elevate

Our mission is to increase patient engagement and satisfaction with high-quality, clinically validated remote care.

—BRONWYN SPIRA, CEO, FORCE THERAPEUTICS

A re you raising a unicorn? I'm referring to tech startups with a $1 billion valuation mark. It's a term coined by Cowboy Ventures founder, Aileen Lee, in a 2013 *TechCrunch* blog post.[30] At the time, a startup with a $1 billion pre-initial public offering (pre-IPO) market value was still considered a fantasy. But just two years later, in 2015, *eighty* private companies had reached the coveted $1 billion mark. That growth trend continued during the digital tech Gold Rush of 2021 as unicorns became increasingly commonplace, numbering over *nine hundred* tech startups worth more than $1 billion. Tech startup investments went crazy that year, reaching $621 billion globally. In the US alone, digital health startups totaled *$29.1 billion* across 729

---

30   Aileen Lee, "Welcome to the Unicorn Club: Learning from Billion-Dollar
       Startups," TechCrunch, November 2, 2013, https://techcrunch.com/2013/11/02/
       welcome-to-the-unicorn-club/.

deals, averaging $39.9 million each.[31] Those numbers have provided a compelling argument for digital tech's investment potential.[32]

Digital health tech was one of the main tech sectors luring investors with the potential of an even larger pot of gold at the end of a startup's valuation rainbow. Not content to run with a herd of unicorns, venture capitalists (VCs) started hunting health-tech startups likely to reach a quick *$10 billion* valuation on their own. That all changed in 2022 when there was a steep drop in US health investment in digital health tech. This meant startups only had access to $15.3 billion, as compared to the previous year's high of $29.1 billion.[33] With the cooling period likely to continue, healthcare remains an industry where tech will help investments come back up.

Corporate decision-makers I talk to want to leverage tech's benefits since all of them continue to have one objective—to improve their businesses. As a healthcare stakeholder, it's likely you're focused on doing that too—working hard to *increase* your company's sales, market share, profitability, and customer loyalty. And you'll undoubtedly be syncing your upward trajectory with simultaneous steps designed to reduce costs, errors, and employee turnover. That means identifying the factors that limit productivity and employee engagement.

31   Adriana Krasniansky, Bill Evans, and Megan Zweig, "2021 Year End: Digital Health Funding Seismic Shifts beneath the Surface," Rock Health, January 5, 2022, https://rockhealth.com/insights/2021-year-end-digital-health-funding-seismic-shifts-beneath-the-surface/.

32   "$1B+ Market Map: The World's 1,206 Unicorn Companies in One Infographic," CB Insights, accessed January 2023, https://www.cbinsights.com/research/unicorn-startup-market-map/.

33   Kyle Bryant, Madelyn Knowles, Adriana Krasniansky, "2022 Year End: Digital Health Funding Lessons at the End of a Funding Cycle," Rock Health, January 11, 2023, https://rockhealth.com/insights/2022-year-end-digital-health-funding-lessons-at-the-end-of-a-funding-cycle/.

In order to see your healthcare company reach its full potential, I have some essential advice for you: your health service or solution will need to lessen the impact of chronic disease.

TARGET CHRONIC DISEASE

The reason I advise companies to focus on developing and adopting tech that fights chronic disease is twofold. *First, chronic disease impacts about half of American adults.*[34] That's why solutions that focus on reducing chronic disease morbidity and mortality—whether in the form of a device or service—are so desperately needed to help this large portion of the patient population. *Second, a large population comprises a huge market for any kind of innovation that offers real benefit.* These two facts are the reason VCs are still hunting for these *unicorns.*

Such investment is based on solid data from organizations like the American Diabetes Association (ADA). The ADA released findings estimating that the total cost of diagnosed diabetes rose by 26 percent in five years, increasing the cost of treating the disease from $245 to $327 billion during that period.[35] In the US, individuals with diagnosed diabetes incur average medical expenditures of $16,752 per year—of which about $9,601 is directly attributed to diabetes. On average, those individuals have medical expenditures approximately 2.3 times higher than what their annual expenses would be without diabetes.[36] In light

---

34 "National Center for Chronic Disease Prevention and Health Promotion," Centers for Disease Control and Prevention, accessed January 2023, https://www.cdc.gov/chronicdisease/index.htm.

35 "New American Diabetes Association Report Finds Annual Costs of Diabetes to be $412.9 Billion," American Diabetes Association, accessed January 2023, https://diabetes.org/about-us/statistics/cost-diabetes.

36 American Diabetes Association, "Economic Costs of Diabetes in the U.S. in 2017," *Diabetes Care* 41, no. 5 (May 2018): 917–928. doi: 10.2337/dci18-0007.

of these staggering costs, it's encouraging to know that type 2 diabetes could be reversed with healthy lifestyle changes.[37] Those changes can be supported by an array of digital health tech, such as mobile health (mHealth), which delivers healthcare via mobile devices, such as cell phones and tablets. One study showed mHealth apps, Twitter, and fitness trackers promoted a healthier lifestyle as those mHealth interventions increased participants' number of steps and vegetable/fruit intake while reducing their sugar-sweetened beverage intake.[38]

That's the good news. The bad news is that refusing to adopt healthy habits or simply delaying type 2 diabetes treatment can cause permanent, irreversible medical consequences. Blindness from diabetic retinopathy, for example, is only one such potential consequence. Nearly 30 percent of diabetics suffer from the condition, which is the leading cause of *preventable* blindness among American adults. Yet, it's 90 percent avoidable with proper diagnosis and treatment.[39] In the fight to prevent diabetic retinopathy, teleretinal imaging is one digital tech tool that's proving to be a powerful ally.

Digital retinal imaging gives a more complete view of potentially irreversible eye changes. Such changes include macular degeneration and glaucoma as well as diabetic retinopathy. With new eye tech like the Intelligent Retinal Imaging System (IRIS), providers *of all types* can screen at-risk diabetes patients with the IRIS teleretinal exam during

---

37   Benjamin R. Brown, "Reversing Chronic Diseases Using Lifestyle Medicine," in *Integrative Preventive Medicine*, ed. Richard H. Camona and Mark Liponis (New York: Oxford Academic Press, 2017).

38   Alexander E. Chung, Asheley C. Skinner, Stephanie E. Hasty, and Eliana M. Perrin, "Tweeting to Health: A Novel mHealth Intervention Using Fitbits and Twitter to Foster Healthy Lifestyles," *Clinical Pediatrics* 56, no. 1 (January 2017): 26–32, https://doi.org/10.1177/0009922816653385.

39   Ryan Lee, Tien Y. Wong, and Charumathi Sabanayagam, "Epidemiology of Diabetic Retinopathy, Diabetic Macular Edema and Related Vision Loss," *Eye and Vision* 2, no. 17 (September 30, 2015), doi: 10.1186/s40662-015-0026-2.

their office visits. This preventive approach to diabetic retinopathy is a good example of how digital health tech can benefit patients, offering better quality-of-life outcomes than traditional approaches.

THE RIGHT TOOL FOR THE JOB

Making quality of life the top priority in patient care may seem unrealistic amid the day-to-day pressures of treating patients in an overburdened health system. But smart stakeholders can support improved quality-of-life metrics for patients by using digital health tech with the following efficiencies:

Tech that prevents or mitigates chronic disease via interactive devices that provide patients with immediate feedback. Sensors, wearables, and virtual assistants help treat chronic disease by encouraging patients to observe and take responsibility for their own health status. As patients track their physiological and psychological symptoms, they receive immediate feedback and become attuned to how their lifestyle choices are impacting them in real time.

Tech that monitors patients remotely via devices that improve disease management by collecting and reporting data to providers. Remote patient monitors allow providers to continuously track the status of patients' health without being physically present. These devices enable providers to oversee more patients while ensuring those patients are adhering to treatments and recovering after acute episodes. An RPM's algorithms can also capture data to prove the benefit of other new health tech the patient is using.

Simply stated, digital health tech is the future of medicine in terms of its treatment, delivery, and payment systems.

As the digital transformation of healthcare unfolds, it's apparent that digital health technology is fueling better patient outcomes. That's the good news. The bad news is that this positive change is happening only at a fraction of the pace possible. Accessing digital tech's full potential is going to require tech pioneers and corporate decision-makers to know something about other healthcare *stakeholders*, the healthcare *ecosystem* itself, and its *payment structures*.

Since the different stakeholders' functions are interactive, they hinge on one another's contributions. When remote monitoring tech prevents a medical crisis, for example, this intervention benefits the patient's health, reduces the hospital system's burden, and potentially generates new revenue sources—while supporting the entire system and reducing costs overall. This is why the various stakeholders all need to know the "bottom line" benefits of new tech as it relates to their own priorities. Pioneers who understand which payers are likely to adopt their innovations will be more aggressive creating and testing it.

HEALTHCARE'S FIVE KEY STAKEHOLDERS

The 5Ps each have their own focus and priorities, but the ultimate goal of all 5P stakeholders is better healthcare quality at lower cost for everyone. After all, patients are the *end users* of healthcare and the reason it exists in the first place.

Patients

Since patients are the stakeholders who actually make use of the goods or services produced by healthcare businesses, they are the stakeholders who are the end users of care in the health system. Most patients pay for it with insurance that divides them into three main patient categories (and some patients do not have insurance coverage):

1. Those with employer-based insurance
2. Those with government program–based insurance
3. Those with private insurance they have to purchase themselves

Patients with employer-based insurance and government program–based insurance often have little choice when it comes to choosing their health plans, but they usually have much more cost-effective coverage because of the negotiating power of their employers and the government. Those who don't have access to either employer or government insurance will have to purchase private insurance. When they do, they're likely to find they have more options in terms of their coverage, costs, and provider networks, but their premiums will usually be higher.

Payers

The primary payers in our healthcare system are health insurance companies, and they're the stakeholders investing most heavily in the digital healthcare revolution. As they do, these investors are undergoing their own transformation in response to VBC and other industry pressures. In order for digital health pioneers, entrepreneurs, and developers to support payers' economic realities, they need to understand the payer stakeholders' four main digital priorities.

Improve the Experience of End Users (Patients)

The Affordable Care Act (ACA) increased direct interaction of insurers with end users (patients) instead of relying solely on brokers and large corporations. Today, healthcare payers must make sure they're providing user-intuitive features and an engaging consumer experience through their devices and channels. The companies Kaiser Permanente and Aviva Health, for example, are using powerful consumer engagement models that leverage mobile tech. One intelligent app they're offering makes the patient experience more convenient by automating prescription refills and providing appointment notifications. The app eliminates the need to wait in long queues to refill prescriptions, and its alerts help avoid missed doctor visits.

COST OF CARE INTRODUCTION

National health care spend continues to increase resulting in the need for payers to manage cost to maintain competitive advantage in the marketplace

> Total Expenses = Cost of Care + Admin

Total Cost of Care refers to the total cost of a population and what it costs to care for them medically, similar to Cost of Goods Sold (CoGS) direct costs of producing goods sold by a company.

Administrative Cost include the expenses associated with running the business including; vendor fees, FTE support and marketing.

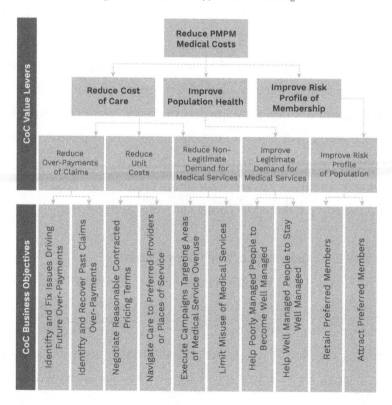

Reduce Costs while Optimizing Operational Efficiency

Ongoing and past healthcare reforms like those of the ACA have required payers to rapidly cover the cost of providing healthcare for millions of new users. Payers have also been forced to cope with the added cost and efficiency challenges posed by Medical Loss Ratio (MLR) enforcement. As explained by CMS,[40] MLR requires health insurance companies (i.e., payers) to limit the amount of premium dollars they spend on administrative costs for overhead, executive salaries, and marketing.

CMS has imposed these restrictions to ensure at least 80–85 percent of the premium dollars consumers pay for their health insurance is actually spent addressing their healthcare needs. Payers who don't comply will have to issue rebates to their beneficiaries when they fail to meet the minimum of these standards. Policymakers have also imposed rate review provisions that limit payers' ability to increase their insurance rates.

Since these constraints force payers to streamline their business processes, it's these constraints that motivate payers to invest in digital tech. One example is the way the care management company Molina uses iPads loaded with patient forms, including those for applications, intake, assessment, and follow-ups. Digitization of customer communication management (CCM) is also minimizing operational costs. And thanks to CMS's approval of telehealth in 2016, payers are keenly aware of how virtual care is optimizing providers' healthcare delivery while lowering costs of remote checkups, treatments, and diagnostics.

---

40   "Medical Loss Ratio," Centers for Medicare and Medicaid Services, accessed January 2023, https://www.cms.gov/CCIIO/Programs-and-Initiatives/Health-Insurance-Market-Reforms/Medical-Loss-Ratio.

UNDERSTAND MEDICAL LOSS RATIO

MLR is closely watched as a gauge of health spending and insurers' operational profitability

$$\frac{\text{Medical Claims + Quality Improvement Expenditures}}{\text{Earned Premiums − Taxes, Licensing and Regulatory Fees}} = \text{MLR}$$

MLR Guidelines*

The Affordable Care Act requires insurers to submit data on proportion of premium revenues spent on clinical services and quality improvement

The Affordable Care Act requires insurance companies to spend at least 80% or 85% of premium dollars on medical care, with the rate review provisions imposing tighter limits on health insurance rate increases. If an issuer fails to meet the applicable MLR standard in any given year, as of 2012, the issuer is required to provide a rebate to its customer.

MLR requirements apply to fully insured small and larger employer groups and individual commercial health plans, including grandfathered plans. They do not apply to self-funded groups to stop-loss coverage.

- Main business objective is to manage medical costs while investing in care of members
- Quality improvement expenditure (aka benefit expenses) allow for investment of premium dollars earned to be put towards enhancing care of members
- Plan premium rate changes are more moderate, since they are used as a benchmark against competitors and impact rebates issues
- Improve efficiencies to reduce operational/admin costs paid by 20% – 15% of generated revenue

* CMS.gov Centers A federal government website managed and paid for by the U.S. Centers for Medicare & Medicaid Services

Understand MLR: The importance of understanding MLR

Collaborate to Implement Connected Health

Payers, providers, pharma companies, and medical-equipment companies are all working together to deliver better, more efficient healthcare at lower cost. To that end, it is likely that providers will be prescribing smartphone apps in the near future—just as they currently do with medications or physical therapy. Hospitals are already enlisting the aid of developers, requesting new mobile apps that can monitor patients and simultaneously convey their medical status back to their doctors in real time. In a different kind of collaboration, insurance startup Oscar rewarded members with Amazon gift cards when members reached set health goals as documented by a free, wearable fitness tracker the company had provided. It was a win-win for both members and payers since company costs went down when members achieved better health using their fitness tracker.

Outcomes versus Profits

The success of these health-tech examples shows why it's important for digital health pioneers to develop tech that supports the three payer priorities I've just described. Identifying which health insurance companies are investing the most aggressively is helpful, too. For many years now, that's been the US government that pays more toward healthcare than any other single entity. Back in 2012, the US Chamber of Commerce Foundation used White House numbers to conclude that almost 65 percent of the US budget was being spent on Medicare and Social Security.[41] Part of that percentage was the $79.9 billion allocated to Health and Human Services (HHS) that year. Ten years later (in 2022), the HHS budget had risen to $131.8 billion in discretionary budget authority and $1.5 trillion in mandatory funding.[42]

> **In other words, the core business of the government isn't primarily about administering justice or foreign policy but providing insurance.**

41   Tom Stanton, "Why the US Government Is Nothing More than an Insurance Company Army," U.S. Chamber of Commerce Foundation, January 10, 2019, https://www.uschamberfoundation.org/blog/post/why-us-government-nothing-more-insurance-company-army/33935.

42   "HHS Budget in Brief FY 2022," U.S. Department of Health and Human Services, accessed January 2023, https://www.hhs.gov/about/budget/fy2022/index.html.

Together, government insurance and private health insurance companies are the payer stakeholders dealing with all the financial elements of the health insurance policy framework. Their primary role is obtaining healthcare services on behalf of their beneficiaries. Financially, that means payers and providers have a customer/supplier relationship. And since patients often have a choice of which insurance payer they want to use, these payers may also have a customer/supplier relationship with their patient beneficiaries.

As government payers, Medicare and Medicaid aren't business enterprises per se, but they're still actively trying to minimize their funding costs just like the for-profit private payers. This cost-saving incentive is motivating both government and private payers to invest in interactive digital health tech that promotes healthy-living initiatives for their beneficiary population. *Smart developers and entrepreneurs will leverage this powerful payer priority, knowing payers want more efficient, high-quality, cost-effective services for their beneficiaries.* Simply put, payers and their beneficiaries want the same thing—they want more for their money.

Of course, private insurance payers are more driven to cut costs for the health benefits packages they offer because they have to remain financially sustainable while conforming to applicable legislative policy. For developers and entrepreneurs, the crucial point here is that increasing numbers of patients/beneficiaries are getting to choose their insurance payer. This is why *it's vital that digital health pioneers know which health tech is trending in popularity and/or what combination of tech patients are likely to value most highly.* Understanding which of the new healthcare tech offerings will benefit the greatest number of patients most effectively—while also lowering payer costs—will be the sweet spot for investors and tech pioneers.

Providers

The term *providers* refers to all stakeholders involved in delivering healthcare services to patients. These may be healthcare facilities, such as hospitals, clinics, nursing homes, and rehabilitation centers, or the healthcare practitioners themselves. Such practitioners include physicians, nurses, therapists, technicians, administrators, and a range of professionals involved in the diagnosis, treatment, and management of a patient's care. Since physicians are a primary part of a patient's care team, they're well positioned to recommend new digital healthcare to patients. For that reason, they play a central role in health tech's adoption.

As providers oversee, coordinate, plan, and deliver health services to patients, many of them deliver healthcare as independent businesses, managing their own operations and finances. Therefore, they may have a direct interest in using innovation that saves time or improves efficiency. And it's why providers continued to use telehealth after the pandemic subsided. Besides its many medical benefits, telehealth became even more attractive to providers when CMS made it reimbursable. Regarding reimbursement, providers are primarily incentivized in the health system to use the following two payment arrangements:

1. *Fees-for-service* to maximize their time and the number of patients they see

2. *Capitation* to receive a fixed fee per the number of patients an insurer assigns them

Besides these two ways to get paid, there are several other ways to get reimbursed, including *episodic bundled care, pay-for-performance,* and *value-based contracts.* Providers aren't limited to using one type of reimbursement either but will often seek payment for their health services to different patients using different reimbursement types—

with each one requiring different billing, coding, and claims-sub-mission processes. While navigating that complexity, many providers have been reluctant to adopt new digital tech because they're already working beyond capacity. Quite a few are also constrained by the following misconceptions:

- Conclusion that digital health tools are "solutions" in search of a problem
- Perception of the difficulty required to change practice protocols
- Confusion about the cost of tech adoption and needed training
- Assumption that AI and health-tech automation will ultimately replace them

It's imperative that tech pioneers understand the provider mindset and their operational constraints before using facts and data to dispel their health-tech misconceptions. By immersing themselves in the provider mindset, pioneers will be able to offer detailed, strategic plans showcasing specific tech in a way that answers providers' five main tech-adoption questions:

1. Will it improve my patient outcomes?
2. Can it reduce my care delivery costs or increase my care delivery revenue?
3. Is it the highest quality for my patient, or will it increase my liability risk?
4. What resources will I have to invest in terms of time, money, and space?
5. How hard will it be to incorporate into the way I run my practice?

Pioneers that do the work to understand provider constraints and pain points will be able to align themselves as partners who are supporting providers' priorities rather than vendors who are simply trying to sell them something. Partnering is an advantage for both the provider and the pioneer. The provider doesn't have to keep assessing crowds of new, untried vendors, and the pioneer can scale their tech to benefit more providers.

Policymakers

Policymakers set the regulatory framework that determines what healthcare US citizens receive. As such, they're the stakeholder that positions the government to either foster or impede new digital tech's adoption and implementation. The fact that federal policymakers, such as CMS, are supportive of upgrading US healthcare with digital health tech is very good news for tech pioneers, providers, payers, and patients. Their positive support is based on population-level data, and metrics that document various types of health tech benefit their constituents in the following ways:

- Increase access to healthcare services that cost less
- Improve quality of delivered care and patient safety
- Optimize care coordination between provider stakeholders
- Support public health with a preventive approach
- Ensure adequate number of healthcare professionals
- Promote research and further innovation

As a federal agency, CMS has prioritized healthcare outcomes instead of stakeholder profits using a VBC approach to overhaul the fragmented American healthcare system. By fragmented, I'm referring to the complex, competing health-sector interests that don't always put patient/consumer interests first. Quarterly earnings often take precedence.

Pioneers

First and foremost, pioneers are visionaries. Some of these pioneers are the healthcare stakeholders developing and marketing digital health tech via startups. I've already described some of their health products and services (more to come) and how they're creating the critically needed technology that's currently transforming healthcare. But when I use the term *pioneer*, I intend that term to encompass *any visionary in healthcare*—and not just entrepreneurs who've developed a specific product or service and started a digital tech company.

Rather, a pioneer is any visionary who identifies ways to improve healthcare's operations and systems. Instead of resigning themselves to a "business as usual" approach, many clinicians and administrators are taking on the role of pioneers. They're doing it by dedicating themselves to improving the efficiency, quality, and delivery of care services within their existing systems. Pioneers upgrade healthcare's *status quo*.

ARE YOU KEEPING UP WITH INNOVATION?

Technical innovation in the realm of digital health is happening *exponentially* as each novel discovery spurs an array of further advancement, including hardware, software, and services for coordinated and managed care. Wearables, for instance, collect comprehensive physical and behavioral user metrics from individual patients that can be used to innovate care delivery and clinical research. Such data can identify people at risk of diseases and improve adherence to treatment. In clinical trials and observational studies, digital data can also be used to measure patient-centered outcomes.

Data is what identifies the relevant factors driving real-world patient outcomes, and it's the factor driving digital innovation in healthcare. Those innovations include mobile health apps, EHRs, wearable devices, telehealth, and telemedicine. And now that the computational wizardry of AI has been incorporated into digital health tech, the innovation genie's out of the bottle.

As the pace of innovation accelerates, some healthcare stakeholders may feel they've been caught off balance. Providers, especially, are feeling the pressure to change their operational workflows to comply with new federal policy changes. Those policies are requiring providers to standardize their healthcare processes—establishing best practices with good outcomes they can actually document. But such standardization also means healthcare providers are being subjected to a new level of scrutiny provided by data mining and other digital evidence proving which processes work and which don't. RPM devices, for example, accomplish that in two ways:

1. **Offer physiologic monitoring to enhance traditional, on-site disease *management***

2. **Provide monitoring that improves health habits and helps *prevent* chronic disease**

RPM in a nonclinical setting, such as a patient's home, can reduce patient travel costs and infection risk. In fact, the Center for Care Transformation at AVIA—a healthcare digital transformation technology and services company—has estimated that for every group of five hundred high-risk Medicare patients with multiple chronic conditions, health systems can obtain $5.2 million in annual cost savings using RPM.[43] We'll talk more about RPM later in chapter 9: Wi-Fi Wellness.

Meanwhile, it's important to note that some analysts claim that adopting and implementing digital health technology is *increasing*

---

43   Bill Siwicki, "How Remote Patient Monitoring Improves Care & Saves Money for Chronic Care," HealthITAnalytics, June 2, 2020, https://www.healthcareitnews.com/news/how-remote-patient-monitoring-improves-care-saves-money-chronic-care.

overall healthcare costs instead of reducing them. They claim we don't need "new widgets" but better processes to increase productivity.[44] I say we need *both*. When implemented properly, digital health-tech innovations *improve* processes throughout the healthcare system. *But tech innovation isn't a magic wand that produces spectacular outcomes instantaneously.* Research and development (R&D) is costly in any industry, and the health sector is no different. That R&D expense occurs up front as does the front-end cost of implementing digital health tech into an existing business model—models that can't cope with the current crisis in the healthcare system. That means the health industry doesn't really have a choice when it comes to adopting health tech. The eventual, cumulative cost savings of increased productivity makes the initial investment *essential*.

THE SHIFTING HEALTH INVESTMENT LANDSCAPE

Smartphones, inexpensive sensors, and cloud computing are all enabling the new connected services that are transforming healthcare. Savvy investors still see solid opportunity in this technology upheaval. And their thinking has proven to be correct. Even though 2023's higher interest rates slowed tech investing overall, *health-tech investments have remained stable.* To prove the point, the top new unicorns in the first quarter of 2023 were Oura ($2.6 billion) and Clarify Health ($1.4 billion). That wasn't a coincidence.

Investors know the health-tech sector represents a stable investment for three obvious reasons:

---

44   Teresa M. Waters and David R. Graf, "Prepare to Be an Employer of Choice for Millennials," Health Affairs Blog, June 25, 2018, https://www.healthaffairs.org/do/10.1377/forefront.20180625.763681/full/.

1. The percentage of older people in the US is growing, so the health industry will too.

2. Stakeholders want to leverage the efficiency and cost benefits of digital health tech.

3. Federal policy is openly mandating the use of health tech to promote VBC.

These health-tech investors know it's crucial to stay informed about the current and *ongoing* development and deployment of digital health tech throughout the industry. They also know it's equally important to understand how long-term socioeconomic factors are impacting the future healthcare landscape.

WHAT LIES AHEAD?

While it's impossible to predict outcomes with 100 percent accuracy, I'm sure of one thing: stakeholders who refuse to innovate won't fare well, as outside players like Google, Amazon, Facebook, Microsoft, and Apple enter the health industry fray. However, these tech giants must understand the implications of deploying its power and potential in healthcare with the 5P stakeholders, especially providers and policymakers.

Ironically, the traditional health sector has been slower than other sectors to adopt digital tech innovation. And that's the case even though its primary stakeholders know change to the healthcare system is desperately needed. Providers and payers who embrace the promise of digital health tech will have access to $1 trillion worth of improvement.[45] But accessing that promise will require redesign-

---

45 Shashank Bhasker, Damien Bruce, Jessica Lamb, and George Stein, "Tackling Healthcare's Biggest Burdens with Generative AI," McKinsey & Company, July 10, 2023, https://www.mckinsey.com/industries/healthcare/our-insights/tackling-healthcares-biggest-burdens-with-generative-ai.

ing their organizations and innovating with new health-tech business models—those that refashion care and reallocate constrained resources to increase productivity.[46] Players that apply these practices to cope with the current healthcare crisis have the opportunity to set themselves up for success in the years ahead.

The way Force, Hinge, and a wide array of healthcare companies are using digital interfaces perfectly illustrates the objectives of VBC and CMS's quality metric goals (as expressed in CMS's Star Ratings). And the nongovernmental quality assessment ratings provided by HEDIS and CQMS (clinical quality measures) are doing the same. The health tech I've just described:

- lowers providers' costs,
- offers increased value to patients and consumers, and
- delivers metrics to prove its efficacy and improved outcomes.

Meeting these goals is important for tech pioneers because there's growing federal pressure to base reimbursement on documented outcomes. Since quality assurance assessments provide "proof of concept," *new health tech with proven metrics will win adoption over less data-driven tech options every time.*

MY EXECUTIVE TAKEAWAY

In order to accelerate the digital technology transformation of healthcare, better collaboration between key stakeholders is essential. By working more closely together, patients, providers, payers, and poli-

---

46 Addie Fleron and Shubham Singhal, "The Gathering Storm: The Uncertain Future of US Healthcare," McKinsey & Company, September 16, 2022, accessed January 2023, https://www.mckinsey.com/industries/healthcare/our-insights/the-gathering-storm-the-uncertain-future-of-us-healthcare.

cymakers all stand to gain by promoting the adoption of digital health technology with the following approach:

> To collaborate more strategically, tech pioneers need to have an entrepreneurial mindset that takes all of the other stakeholders' perspectives and pain points into account.

> Since each of these players has different motivations, interests, and constraints, pioneers and corporate decision-makers need to understand the priorities of the other stakeholders, payment structures, and the healthcare ecosystem itself.

> Proceed knowing the healthcare ecosystem functions in an environment where stakeholders want to maintain balance between access, quality, and cost containment in order to achieve value.

Traditionally, the healthcare industry has focused on achieving operational efficiency to lower costs and increase efficiency, but that isn't sufficient. We need to focus and invest more into innovation to stay competitive and to truly improve our current model of care delivery. In the next chapter, I'll show you how to unleash innovation's value drivers.

REVVING UP HEALTHCARE

Unleashing Innovation's Value Drivers

The way to transform healthcare is to realign competition with value for patients. Value in healthcare is the health outcome per dollar of cost expended. If all system participants have to compete on value, value will improve dramatically.

—MICHAEL E. PORTER, PROFESSOR, HARVARD BUSINESS SCHOOL

I know the pioneers founding health-tech startups aim to save the day as they create the novel solutions so desperately needed in a fragmented US health system. As they do, they're also aiming to disrupt the health industry in a way that generates an astronomical return on investment (ROI). But disrupting the health industry isn't easy. It means creating innovation that changes traditional thinking and business practices with an entirely new health-delivery *template*. An obvious example is the way telemedicine has increasingly shifted care away from in-person provider visits to remote consultations. It's also evident in the way RPM is moving post-acute recovery in hospitals to patients' homes instead. More rapid iteration is driving continuous product improvement and delivering scale beyond helping thousands of people to helping millions and the healthcare system itself.

THE VALUE OF PREVENTION

As 5P stakeholders align to develop, adopt, and implement the use of digital health tech for disease prevention, they will help reverse the chronic disease epidemic in the US by lessening (or even preventing) the following five risk factors that are the well-known *precursors* of patients' chronic diseases:

1. **Tobacco use/smoke exposure**
2. **Poor nutrition**
3. **Excessive alcohol**
4. **Physical inactivity**
5. **Lack of sleep**

In the case of tobacco use, for example, smoking cigarettes is the leading preventable cause of disease, disability, and death in the US. It harms nearly every organ of the body, causing cancer, heart disease, stroke, lung diseases, and type 2 diabetes.[47] For every person who dies because of smoking, at least thirty more people are living with a serious smoking-related illness, a group totaling 16 million Americans.[48] Even back in 2018, the price tag for smoking in the US was over $600 billion.[49]

To prevent loss of life and the massive costs associated with smoking and the other four precursors of chronic disease, a digital health-tech prevention approach has been endorsed by CMS and many other health-space players. *Most importantly*, focusing on prevention of various unhealthy habits or choices will create a better

---

47   "Smoking & Tobacco Use: Impact on Population," Centers for Disease Control and Prevention, accessed January 2023, https://www.cdc.gov/chronicdisease/programs-impact/pop/tobacco.htm.

48   Ibid.

49   Ibid.

quality of life for patients. The only remaining question is *how*. Fortunately, digital health tools have been designed to do just that—help patients fight and win against the health habits that lead to, or worsen, chronic disease. The examples that follow are just a sample of the growing trove of digital health-tech tools.

Risk Factor 1: Tobacco Use and Exposure to Secondhand Smoke

Digital smoking cessation tools and/or products can harness behavioral health data—including craving patterns, stressors, and smoking routines, such as the digital transdermal patch that releases nicotine at timed intervals when cravings are known to be strongest. Since data indicates 75 percent of smokers have their first cigarette within thirty minutes of waking up, this digital nicotine replacement therapy (NRT) provides support before the morning craving strikes.[50]

Risk Factor 2: Poor Nutrition

Viewing food as medicine is smart, because prioritizing food and diet helps prevent, reduce, or reverse disease. Changing eating habits is hard. So the Community Preventive Services Task Force (CPSTF) is promoting healthy eating in workplaces using health information digitally shared through computers, websites, mobile apps, text messages, emails, or phone calls. Evidence from a systematic review of seventeen studies showed the interventions increased fruit and vegetable intake, decreased fat intake, and improved or maintained

---

50 "Smoking Cessation Tools in the Digital Health Space," Smoking Cessation Leadership Center, University of California San Francisco, accessed January 2023, https://smokingcessationleadership.ucsf.edu/news/smoking-cessation-tools-digital-health-space.

weight. Computer-generated feedback that provided tailored information through each of these communication platforms did the same.[51]

Risk Factor 3: Excessive Alcohol Use

Apps like DrinkControl are available to either track users' alcohol consumption or help them maintain sobriety. The app DrinkCoach also offers users the in-app ability to consult a professional "drink coach." Another easy-to-use app, NOMO, helps users count the days they've been sober as motivation. SoberTime does that too but offers a built-in community for additional support. Such help is also provided by multiple apps like Joe & Charlie or the 12 Steps AA Companion that supports AA's twelve-step program. Wearables are helping too. A wristband device called Skyn calculates the body's alcohol content (BAC) forty-five minutes after drinking and displays it on the wristband. ION™ is another inconspicuous wearable that provides continuous alcohol consumption monitoring. These wearable alcohol trackers are helpful because they provide drinkers with more objective measures of alcohol use than their own perception.

Risk Factor 4: Physical Inactivity

Consumers are most familiar with fitness apps tracking their weight-loss efforts with smartwatches, diet-monitoring websites, and digital scales. User engagement is key. Analysis shows that users who tracked their diet or physical activity with digital tools did so more consistently

---

51   "Nutrition and Physical Activity: Worksite Digital Health and Telephone Interventions to Increase Healthy Eating and Physical Activity," health.gov, accessed January 2023, https://health.gov/healthypeople/tools-action/browse-evidence-based-resources/nutrition-and-physical-activity-worksite-digital-health-and-telephone-interventions-increase-healthy-eating-and-physical-activity.

and stayed more engaged than those using more traditional means, such as handwritten records of exercise routines or calorie intake.[52]

Risk Factor 5: Lack of Sleep

Despite the wide variety of sleep trackers currently available, new versions are still being developed. Some are wearables worn on the wrist, while others clip onto your pillow or sit next to your bed. These devices typically track the following different aspects of sleep:[53]

- *Duration of sleep* is recorded by tracking when you're inactive.
- *Quality of sleep* is tracked by identifying movements linked to interrupted sleep.
- *Phases of sleep* are monitored using movement to detect when sleep is less deep.
- *Environmental factors* like temperature or light level are recorded.
- *Lifestyle factors* affecting sleep such as caffeine, mealtime, or stress can be entered.

Some apps screen people online, connect them to virtual sleep specialists, and provide at-home testing, treatment, and personalized coaching to promote better sleep.[54] Better than only measuring *movements* to infer quality, next-generation sleep monitors measure

---

52   Stanford Medicine, "Digital Health Tracking Tools Help Individuals Lose Weight, Study Finds," February 2, 2021, https://med.stanford.edu/news/all-news/2021/02/digital-health-tracking-tools-help-individuals-lose-weight-study-finds.html.

53   "Do Sleep Trackers Really Work?" Johns Hopkins Medicine, accessed January 2023, https://www.hopkinsmedicine.org/health/wellness-and-prevention/do-sleep-trackers-really-work.

54   Nick Paul Taylor, "ResMed, Google Sibling Verily Form Digital Health Venture to Improve Access to Sleep Treatment," MedTech Dive, December 15, 2021, https://www.medtechdive.com/news/resmed-RMD-verily-GOOGL-sleep-disorders-digital-health-joint-venture/636555/.

brain waves in addition to analyzing the stages of a person's sleep cycle during the night.

The cost savings of those devices and sleep apps versus sleep lab testing are substantial. Most apps are free to download onto various devices. And even though the apps typically require a monthly subscription of $5–$10 a month for ongoing access, that's minimal compared to the costs of in-lab sleep tests that may range from $2,646 to $19,334.[55]

Digital health tech's potential ability to manage patients' chronic diseases more effectively and affordably, and prevent it in the first place, continues to increase its value for stakeholders.

Paying less to treat fewer cases of chronic disease is the only way forward in healthcare.

HOW TO APPROACH THOSE YOU WANT TO CONVINCE

No matter how effective pioneers' innovations may be, the ebb and flow of market forces will shape how payers and providers respond to new tech. Pioneers seeking investment dollars must understand *current* and *projected* market forces, their competitors, and the durability of their new tech's *proven* usefulness to different stakeholders' interests. As I mentioned previously, that requires understanding the mindsets of the other four primary stakeholders.

---

55   Michelle Andrews, "Enough to Wreck Their Rest: $10,322 for a Sleep Study," Kaiser Health News, February 25, 2022, https://khn.org/news/article/enough-to-wreck-their-rest-10322-for-a-sleep-study/.

DIGITAL HEALTHCARE COMPANIES FRAMEWORK

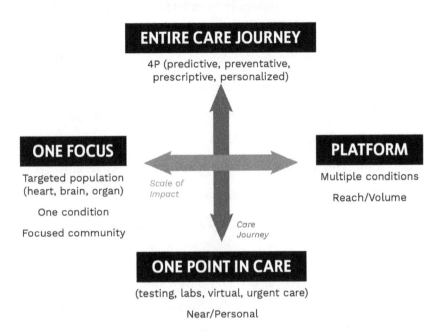

Digital Healthcare Companies Framework: Tech pioneers need to consider if their solution meets a point-of-care need or if it's useful for the entire care journey and if it's right for a platform versus a focused health category.

This knowledge of stakeholders' priorities and pain points will help you know *who* (which investor stakeholder) to approach and *when* to approach them. Understanding how stakeholders interact in the healthcare ecosystem is always essential but even more so during a cooler, slower, and more conservative investment climate. Rising interest rates and tepid consumer interest are just two of the possible reasons for such a climate.

At such times, there's even less room for error, so tech pioneers need to be able to create business cases showing how their digital health solutions prevent or manage chronic disease by answering the following questions:

- Why would other stakeholders be interested in buying/using my tech?
- What ongoing problem(s) does my tech solve for any of them?
- How many competing products are already in development?
- What's unique about my health-tech innovation compared to other solutions?
- How is my solution better, and how have I proved its efficacy?
- Can it get government approval?
- What government policies and agencies are needed to approve my new tech?

Once you can *demonstrate* you have those answers, you'll still need to know *which* investor to approach and how to actually meet with them. That requires networking. In other words, *it's who you know* that's going to be key to your tech-marketing success. That all-important truth wasn't mentioned in the coursework for my MBA degree. But I eventually found out (the hard way) that connecting with the right person via *networking* is all important. Once you have a demonstrably effective piece of health tech, you still have to know whom to call to get to the person who can make the right introductions or decisions.

HOW TO JOURNEY INTO THE HEALTHCARE SPACE

Quite a few of us working in healthcare have spoken with tech pioneers wanting to find investors. But many of those pioneers simply *don't know what they don't know*. I was in that position myself when I was building my own startup. Pioneers need advice from experts at digital health-tech companies on the leading edge. Kathryn Rowerdink is one such authority. A clinical strategist and care delivery expert, she's the kind of expert I wish I'd had access to starting out. When I asked her what tech pioneers most needed to know, she provided the following bankable insights:

1. Find and Take an Easy-to-Hold Space

What do we mean by an "easy-to-hold space"? Choose an area of potential in the health industry that's not attracting every other tech pioneer. Because innovation is happening fast, whatever tech you're developing, someone else is there too. The availability of undeveloped tech space will shrink when you get close to the leading edge where the crowd of competitors thins out. More technical challenges will have to be solved near that leading edge, but the payoff is likely to be exponentially greater too. Facebook is a great example of that—how the "first one through the gate wins."

It's imperative to pay attention to what other developers are doing. Investors often know better than most what's going on behind closed doors. So again, success as a pioneer will largely depend on who and what you know. Accelerators really help with that. The difficulty will be finding one that knows what you don't.

2. If You're Going to Fail, Fail Fast

Knowing when it's time to stop is essential to early momentum. You have to stay fluid and be adaptable if the market shifts after you've started down a particular tech-development path. You don't want to get locked in too early or lose any of your options to pivot in another direction. If you start down a path that's constrained with oligopoly players or regulations, cut your losses. Winning in health tech requires strategizing about which innovation space you can claim while you build up your resources. The tech-development area you choose should be defendable and allow for ease of expansion.

DIGITAL CONTINUUM

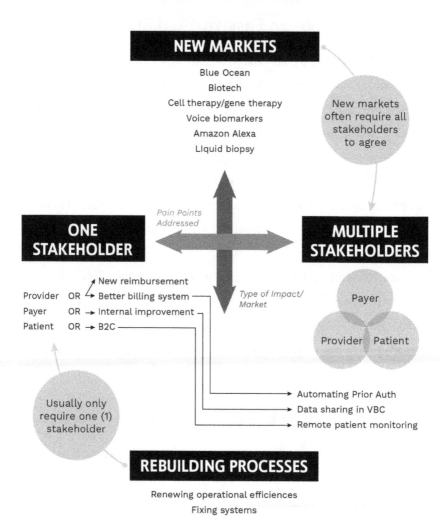

The Digital Continuum includes two types of companies: those that rebuild healthcare processes and those that enter into new markets.

3. Adapt, Adapt, and Adapt Some More

When the situation changes in the business ecosystem, so should you. When market preferences, needs, and industry players change, you need to be ready to adapt—and *fast*. At the same time, it's OK to stay committed to a decision you made in the past. You'll need to assess that conclusion honestly to verify you're not committing a sunk-cost fallacy based on all you've already invested in your present trajectory.

4. Don't Get Too Comfortable

Everyone likes feeling secure, but trying to stay in your comfort zone is a bad thing if you're trying to develop innovative health tech close to the leading edge. Hinge Health, for instance, started with digital physical therapy for musculoskeletal issues. But they later expanded into pelvic health since it complemented what they'd already built in terms of technology. Another decision driver was the fact that there were very few pelvic health solutions in the market. It's important to celebrate small wins. But moving quickly to grab advantage only works if you follow through using the advantage you gained through a previous win.

5. Use Your Mission to Guide Key Decisions

Keep an eye on your mission and your vision before choosing to expand or extend into new spaces. Do *not* expand conceptually if you're unable to execute and show alignment. You must provide evidence and earn the right to defend it. Stay true to your mission and vision, but don't let it blind you to other pioneers and incumbents.

Pick your space and allies based on those that are significant to your mission. Use that focus as the basis for your intentional choice to enter or expand into a market. And pay attention to signals that indicate market changes. Some get nervous after winning a new space and become either overly defensive and conservative or hyperaggressive on multiple fronts. Don't forgo new opportunities, and also don't delude yourself into thinking that every space in healthcare is yours to own.

6. Protect Your Borders

When you've entered a market, you'll have many overlaps and interactions with other startups' solutions that are complementary and aligned. That's a good thing. But you'll encounter others that are in direct competition. The goal is to maximize the solutions that are complementary and aligned to your startup's purpose in order to create synergies that minimize threats to your solution. Once you start expanding, however, the interactions with potential rivals can get complicated fast.

That's why you may first realize the need to establish and maintain market boundaries after your company has expanded too far. It typically happens after a company decides to spin off parts of the business to "focus and prioritize." Although this "belt-tightening" action may look like you're shrinking your business, it tends to strengthen your strategic flexibility and operational focus. This enables you to pursue specific market opportunities more successfully, collaborate with other companies, and better meet customer needs. Operating in too many different spaces does just the opposite. The thinner you stretch yourself, the more at risk all your solutions become. Focusing on expansion needs to be balanced with a core market base.

7. Alliances Offer Powerful Benefits for Health Systems

With any industry, there are going to be companies that pull ahead or have already gotten a head start in a particular space. Trying to compete head-to-head with them is often not as effective as forging an alliance.

This is critical to staying adaptable and impactful with your solution's deployment. The more effectively you do that, the more you'll be able to improve the health of individuals, families, and communities.

It really does take a village to transform healthcare, so try to form alliances with those companies that have visions and missions aligned to your own. Stay vigilant and course correct as needed. Alliances will always be shifting, and you'd be well advised not to dwell on it, take it personally, or resist such changes. Many times, alliances are based on temporary needs, convenience, options, and timing. So you should expect them to change often.

8. Don't Draw Attention to Yourself

Many of the most successful companies in the health industry stay behind the scenes yet still enable the core of the healthcare system to function. There's a reason for that. When companies make it too obvious they're winning in a specific space, other companies may form an alliance with their competitors to level the playing field. That's why flying beneath the radar is underappreciated as a long-term, intentional decision.

Absolutely promote your solution and value. But find the right tone and balance so that you don't appear to be a threat to those in complementary spaces. You can do that by expanding and extending your boundaries at an unobtrusive pace that doesn't make complementary players close ranks. It's much easier to grow if you can avoid attention and remain anonymous until your startup is big enough to be resilient.

9. Know How Your Tech Solution Is Novel

It's vital you know what problem you're solving and how your new health-tech solution is different from your competitors'. Continuous glucose monitors (CGMs), for example, are devices that solve the issue of diabetics having to prick their fingers to test their blood glucose. CGMs track blood sugar using a sensor under the skin. It wirelessly connects to an external transmitter that streams data about a person's blood sugar to an external reader device. It's been a welcome innovation for those with type 2 diabetes, and a lot of competitors have entered that space. Dexcom CGM is just one of those. Although the competition is a boon to consumer choice, it's a problem for health-tech developers.

Here's why: when a lot of companies are offering the same (or similar) solution for the same problem, the solution becomes a commodity that's likely to generate a price war rather than profits. To be useful/successful, a product needs to be different, and stakeholders need to know why that difference matters to patients, providers, payers, policymakers, and their ROI. That requires doing research on competitors and building a business case showing how your solution is superior. Tech incubators and accelerators can help a pioneer who doesn't know where to start. Technical and business know-how are two different skill sets, but both are essential to developing digital health tech. If industry competitors know you have a product similar to their own, it's likely they'll try to beat you to the finish line to market the tech more affordably. Of course, they'll gain market share while doing so.

MY EXECUTIVE TAKEAWAY

The value and benefit of new digital health products on the market has caused a surge of energy throughout the entire industry. Exciting technical leaps keep inspiring even more innovation. Offering novel digital solutions helps advance the entire healthcare industry as people see and experience new, better ways to restore and attain good health.

That's exactly what happened when Hinge Health and Force Therapeutics made physical therapy programs available through interactive online platforms. The success of these two digital platforms is just an indicator of the many startups that are continuing to thrive and grow their market share. To succeed as a tech pioneer, your answer to the following questions should be *yes*:

- *Will the startup team exert maximum effort to develop their concept?* Can they put in the time? If not, others will beat them to the investment finish line, no matter how outstanding it is. Execution is everything.

- *Do you have domain expertise as the founder?* Investors will expect you and your team to know everything about the space in which you're innovating.

- *Is there a significant need for you to develop this idea now?* Market research should show a projected demand for a health-care gap that's not currently being met. Your product or service should also lead in development.

- *Does your big idea have a big-enough market?* The size of the market for your concept will ultimately decide the potential for your idea overall. While obsessing over a niche technol-ogy, a company may beat out their rivals but ultimately fail. That's because a puny market may yield financial outcomes too meager for a startup to thrive (or even survive).

Answering all of the preceding questions with a resounding "yes" means a startup has a shot at becoming part of the 10 percent of early-stage companies that have demonstrated the needed survival skills. That percentage is likely to go even higher if pioneers can show they have a basic understanding of stakeholder competition I'll discuss in the chapter ahead. To help pioneers and startups navigate those business crosscurrents, I'll explain how and why that's happening in the chapter ahead.

STAKEHOLDER SAFARI

Fearless Navigation through the Business Minefield

A little-appreciated barrier to technology innovation involves technology itself—or, rather, innovators' tendency to be infatuated with their own gadgets and blind to competing ideas.

—REGINA E. HERZLINGER, HARVARD BUSINESS SCHOOL

The at-home colon cancer–screening FIT test offered by Everlywell is an excellent example of a breakthrough healthcare technology that's been developed and brought to market in a smart way. This is a noninvasive, at-home screening test for colon and rectal cancer that detects the presence of blood in stool. The test acts like a screening "safety net" for those who might not want a traditional colonoscopy. But what about the other 5P stakeholders? Let's use this test as an example to show some of the typical stakeholder crosscurrents that compete for dominance in our free-market healthcare system. Each stakeholder has their own "angle" and set of priorities. That means there will be a stakeholder "tug of war" every time an innovation comes on the healthcare scene. Whether you run a drug manufacturing company or you own or plan to start a digital health company, you need to understand how the system works.

Because the 5P stakeholders all have a financial stake in the business of healthcare, every innovation may be viewed as a threat to the status quo. Competing interests form a constantly shifting ecosystem with the potential to disrupt one or all of the other stakeholders' interests. That being said, it doesn't have to be an all-out war where one stakeholder loses and another one wins the day.

Despite financial competition between different health-industry stakeholders, each one wins if they pursue the objective of preventing chronic illness. Prioritizing prevention using digital health tech is the goal that will maximize the value of every stakeholder dollar spent. Ultimately, this focus enables the entire healthcare system to save resources, expend less effort, and achieve better health outcomes.

Using Everlywell's at-home colon cancer FIT test as an example, you can see how it might help or hinder the immediate business interests of health industry stakeholders. What about payers? Since Medicare is the biggest one, they clearly opted in, because the test was shown to be effective, efficient, and affordable and was a HEDIS measure. The test is accurate coupled with a higher (potential) patient acceptance rate. Private payers will spend a lot less too, since it is inexpensive compared to a traditional colonoscopy. But unlike a colonoscopy, the FIT test cannot remove any growths in a patient's colon or allow a doctor to visually examine their colon. So if the at-home test indicates the presence of cancer, a colonoscopy would be needed to examine patients endoscopically—which means patients will be going to see their gastroenterologist.

Since many of the people who are reluctant to undergo a colonoscopy will opt to be screened with the at-home test, it gives gastroenterologists another valuable clinical tool to help more patients get screened. And it's the kind of tool that makes it easy to demonstrate a good patient outcome using the CMS value-based criteria. In this one example of stakeholder tension, it's easy to see how and why stakeholders can restrict innovation by seeing it as a threat to their respective spheres of operation. Understanding the various stakeholder mindsets can help prevent defensive/offensive postures that ultimately hurt *all* stakeholders and the healthcare system itself.

HOW STAKEHOLDERS INTERACT

Healthcare stakeholders that collaborate rather than compete can focus on optimizing delivery of care to patients while also working to reach their business goals. That collaborative approach is essential as healthcare's costs continue to rise, and an increasingly fragmented health system seems to be growing more complicated by the day. EHRs are helping, but the transition from paper to digital has been rough. A labyrinth of complicated federal and state policies has tried to streamline the process. But without digital help, manual effort can't parse the mountain of legislation needed to regulate healthcare.

Yes, I admit it—healthcare isn't always user-friendly, efficient, or effective. That's why the solutions offered by digital health-tech pioneers are so desperately needed. Unfortunately, the interplay of stakeholder interests and the healthcare system itself tends to create barriers to tech's creation and implementation. Identifying these issues and the way they impact tech development will enable pioneers to manage them in a way that won't impede innovation. The following chart shows how the different 5P stakeholders deal with cost, experience, outcomes, and brand/reputation factors on two levels:

1. Surface talk—the expected one-liners people say
2. Real talk—pain points and constraints to solve

HEALTHCARE VALUE DRIVERS

Surface Talk

5 PS	COST OF CARE	EXPERIENCE	HEALTH OUTCOMES	QUALITY OF CARE	REPUTATION
Providers	Quality of care, low margins, and not paid well	Admin takes time I should spend with patients	Patient behavior makes change difficult	Always improving	Caring expert
Patients	Complex and no transparency, so just tell me what it will cost	Make it easy, simple, and how I want it (convenient)	Need more help to change my behavior	Give me the best care	Uses Dr. Google too much
Payers	Appropriate care	Doing the best we can under existing constraints, regulations, and more	We change health outcomes through VBC, network, case management, and more	Provide incentives for quality and VBC	Passive stakeholder that provides transactional payments
Pioneers	Innovation will drive down medical costs	Best experience equals best outcomes/value	Better technology will create better health for everyone	Innovation is iterative, but regulatory and legal systems are slowing progress	Disruptive innovation is transforming healthcare
Policymakers (Govt.)	Transparency reduces fraud/abuse Holds healthcare companies (insurer, pharma, etc.) accountable	Improve accessibility for people	Improve outcomes for Healthy People by 2030	Decrease disparities	Aspirational goals

Healthcare Value Drivers chart

Real Talk

5 PS	COST OF CARE	EXPERIENCE	HEALTH OUTCOMES	QUALITY OF CARE	REPUTATION
Providers	Not in my control	Not enough time to care for patients; experience driven by influence on revenue	Patients are not compliant; I can only do my job	I am trained and know what I am doing; I don't need additional oversight	Burnt out, can't focus on healing patients
Patients	Fear medical expense, so delay care because of complexity	Delayed care may result in more aggressive treatment and higher costs	Too expensive, not enough help and resources create frustration	My doctor is a "doctor"; they should know what they are doing, right? What does Google say?	Uses Dr. Google too much—self diagnosing
Payers	Reduce medical spend	Burnt out and frustrated	Improve outcomes that relate to one year ROI	Cost analysis prior to decision and/or mandate from the government	Huge stakeholder (lobbying power) and influence on what is covered, paid for, and amount paid
Pioneers	Doesn't matter, it will come over time or "what is the cost of care and why does it matter to me?"	Over generalized; never actually experienced the realities of the healthcare system	Lack of peer reviewed & published data on clinical efficacy	What exactly is quality of care in new technology?	Trying to build and scale at same time without compelling evidence
Policymakers (Govt.)	Reduce medical trends, not sustainable to continue to pay more	Slow change because of process of regulation change	No idea what to do; try incentives, punish, laws	Regulations and laws are oftentimes increasing care deserts and decreasing access	Controlled by lobbying

Healthcare Value Drivers chart

INNOVATION CROSSCURRENTS

Digital health tech is preventing chronic disease and managing preexisting disease better and more affordably, so why isn't it being more widely implemented? The answer is that competing interests throughout the health industry are suppressing change. Inpatient hospitals and outpatient care providers compete for patients, and the competing interests of different stakeholders may be hard to discern. In other words, these interactions are fluid and will keep shifting as new alliances, partnerships, or perceived adversaries arise. This is why health-tech pioneers must identify the complex priorities of the different stakeholders impacted by their new tech and try to reconcile those priorities with their own.

> **Players in the business of healthcare, as in games of strategy, are either allies or foes with the power to promote or subdue innovation.**

In the case of at-home tests, for example, some hospitals undoubtedly view this as a threat. The reason? It could eliminate traditional revenue. The takeaway here is that pioneers must identify, consult with, negotiate, or ally themselves with the players (read: power brokers) in a given healthcare space or risk failure. One example is the way providers also have turf warfare over patient services with pioneers and among one another. On the funding side, payers will contend with medical service and technology providers over which treatments and payments they'll reimburse for.

Because legislation enacted by policymakers regulates the use of new tech within the healthcare industry, pioneers need to know which network of regulations will affect their innovations. Pioneers must identify who is enacting, revising, and applying relevant policy and how they're doing it. Existing orphan drug laws, for example, that incentivize companies to develop rare disease treatments show how government policy can aid innovation.

> **Tech pioneers may dream of revolutionizing health-care with their groundbreaking innovations, but other health-sector stakeholders will have something to say about that: either helping or hindering pioneers' efforts.**

Since many of these players have the clout to impact public policy and public opinion, they'll promote or attack a particular innovation based on their own special interests. So pioneers need to understand who is benefiting from the status quo and whose toes they're going to be stepping on when their tech is deployed in the market. The potential of digital health tech to save lives makes it all worth it. The at-home FIT cancer test I mentioned previously is a good example, showing how digital tech has the potential to reboot healthcare.

DIGITAL REBOOT REMINDERS

Thanks to the $59.3 billion invested in US health-tech innovation from 2019 to 2022, medical innovation has made incredible technical advances.[56] Yet, all too many of these innovations fail, losing billions of investor dollars in the process. Those failures have a lot to do with competing business interests and a tech pioneer's inability to turn healthcare competitors into allies by demonstrating mutual benefit.

Always keep in mind that the different 5P stakeholders deal with cost, experience, outcomes, and brand/reputation factors on two levels:

56　Kyle Bryant, Madelyn Knowles, Adriana Krasniansky, "2022 Year End: Digital Health Funding Lessons at the End of a Funding Cycle," Rock Health, January 11, 2023, https://rockhealth.com/insights/2022-year-end-digital-health-funding-lessons-at-the-end-of-a-funding-cycle/.

> ➢ Surface talk—the expected one-liners people say
>
> ➢ Real talk—pain points and constraints to solve

Beyond altruism, the health industry is a business, and quarterly reports will dictate the fate of pioneers' efforts. It's not enough to lead the technical pack with a superior product that accomplishes what it says it will—you'll also need to network strategically in light of corporate interests. This requires using strategic business acumen to navigate the complex business environment of competing stakeholder priorities. Understanding that business ecosystem is going to be key to ensuring your solution's success. For those that already have, I'll show how their digital health tech is revolutionizing healthcare.

BYTE-SIZED BREAKTHROUGHS

Now that AI is everywhere in the digital tech world, it's difficult for those of us working in health to remember the time before COVID-19 when telemedicine was seen as a futuristic concept. Although telemedicine's been around since the 1940s, remote care wasn't widely accepted until it was adopted by stakeholders as a measure to limit the spread of the virus during the pandemic. Now it's here to stay, as both patients and providers welcome the convenience, efficiency, and better healthcare access it affords. But telemedicine is just the proverbial "tip of the iceberg" in terms of digital health's many practical, proven, and cost-effective solutions.

Since the pandemic, patients and consumers have become more aware of their own health status and increasingly open to trying digital tech to improve it. Some of the affordable consumer health technology that's already gone mainstream include the following examples:

- **Activity-tracking smartwatches and internet-connected home exercise machines encouraging people to work out more**

- Nutrient-counting apps and self-improvement apps fostering better eating habits
- Websites offering reviews of providers, filling prescriptions, and presenting a wide array of customized healthcare options
- AI-powered virtual assistants giving consumers convenient 24/7 access to healthcare expertise

Patients and consumers have also found *online symptom checkers, patient portals,* and *RPM devices* beneficial too. The result has been an increased demand for personal health monitoring via wearable tech.[57] These devices blur the distinction between consumer and medical technology, especially now that wearable-device vendors have added features for heart rate variability, electrocardiography, pulse oximeters, and continuous glucose monitoring.

Now that digital health tech has moved beyond the hospital, it's aiding the efforts of overworked providers by prompting patients to make healthier lifestyle choices. But whether it's used inside or outside of hospitals, this tech-propelled trend toward prevention represents a more holistic, person-centered approach to wellness—one that fosters better health and social equity as never before. The bottom line is that digital health tech facilitates the prevention of chronic disease. And it's doing so by enhancing the individual patient's sense of personal efficacy, helping them avoid the precursors to chronic disease we discussed earlier.

Preventive efforts to intercede *before* disease develops are the key to replacing the mostly fragmented, *reactive* healthcare system we've known. With so many products becoming available, consumers and patients would be well advised to discuss these new options with their

---

57   "Latest Trends in Medical Monitoring Devices and Wearable Health Technology (2023)," Insider Intelligence, accessed January 2023, https://www.insiderintelligence. com/insights/wearable-technology-healthcare-medical-devices/.

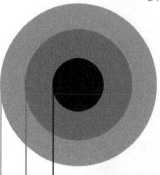

HIGH-PERFORMING DIGITAL ECOSYSTEM

TECHNOLOGY

- Portal
- IoT
- AR/VR
- Kiosk
- Voice
- Med. device/ Digital med.
- Digital Wallet
- Content Management
- Genomics
- Web
- Wearables
- Mobile
- Third-Party
- CRM

TOUCHPOINT

- Employer
- Broker/ben. consumer
- Provider
- Hospital
- Caregiver
- Pharmacist
- CSR
- Plan agent
- Adviser
- Clinic attendant
- Care manager
- Pharma
- Claims reviewer

CAPABILITY

- Enroll/renewal
- Health and wellness
- Rewards
- Health record
- Care search/ transparency
- Care mgmt./ population health
- Rx/pharmacy
- Concierge/ customer service
- Finances
- Social
- Behavioral Health
- Triage and treatment
- Telehealth
- Provider connection
- Chonic/ complex/care support
- Retail/ eCommerce
- Chatbox/ virtual assistant
- Manage plan

Source: "The Imperative for a Consumer-Centric, Digitally Enabled Health Ecosystem," www2.deloitte.com, 2018, https://www2.deloitte.com/content/dam/Deloitte/us/ Documents/life-sciences-health-care/us-lshc-the-digital-imperative.pdf.

High-Performing Digital Ecosystem: Stakeholders can leverage these different types of technology through patient touchpoints and the capabilities needed to enable those touchpoints. [Source: Deloitte Consulting] healthcare providers. It's a wise approach for both eager tech adopters and those suffering from the kind of "information paralysis" that's made them hesitant to try new healthcare technologies. Fortunately, the most effective inducement for reluctant tech adopters is already in their pockets and purses: their smartphones.

DIGITAL TECH IN ACTION

Smartphones have become a vital component for providers too. Physicians who've embraced new digital health tech can link wirelessly to treat many kinds of medical issues. In 2021, for example, the Cleveland Clinic ranked a smartphone-based pacemaker device as a top innovation.[58] When patients used the Medtronic smartphone-based heart device app, MyCareLink Heart, they were more likely to adhere to their data transmission schedule with app-connected devices as opposed to traditional bedside monitors. This adherence is so critical to effective care that research shows it may increase patients' survival rates and also decrease their number of emergency room (ER) visits and the length of their hospital stays.[59]

Using a mobile app, the device can securely and wirelessly transmit data to a patient network. It displays health data from their pacemaker and also transmits it to their physicians. When used in conjunction with a mobile app, this Bluetooth-enabled pacemaker device allows patients to remotely transmit data using their smartphone or tablet. The fact that the pacemaker bypasses the need for additional monitors is a really huge breakthrough. I say that because this breakthrough

---

58 "Top 10 Medical Innovations for 2021," Innovations, Cleveland Clinic, accessed January 2023, https://innovations.clevelandclinic.org/Media/Innovations-Spotlight/Top-10-for-2021-3-Smartphone-Connected-Pacemaker-D.

59 "Connected Heart Devices Named Top Innovation for 2021," Medtronic, accessed January 2023, https://news.medtronic.com/connected-heart-devices-named-top-innovation.

comes at a time when clinical monitoring is critically important to the millions of people who rely on surgically implanted devices like pacemakers to keep them alive.

BETTER SOLUTIONS TO CHRONIC HEALTH PROBLEMS

The digital health services provided by telehealth and telemedicine have proven to be effective solutions to one (or more) of the "Big Five" health problems plaguing Americans: *diabetes, cancer, cardiovascular, musculoskeletal,* and *mental health issues.* Physicians agree these problems aren't going away, so the fact that digital health technology is helping patients with these conditions, while also lowering costs for payers, is a really big deal. That's especially true at a time when many people are struggling to find adequate, affordable care in our existing healthcare system.

It's a huge dilemma that's growing worse—not just in the US but around the world as well. While healthcare costs continue to rise, a growing shortage of physicians is compounding the problem. I've experienced that myself when seeking medical care. Fortunately, digital *telehealth* services are allowing better access to physicians and presenting a welcome, more convenient alternative to in-person consultations.

THE FUNDING PROBLEM

Despite these successes, many promising health-tech products have been killed off because people wouldn't actively use them or because the brilliant solutions they provided weren't able to prove a convincing return to investors. The problem is that we don't always consider how all this innovation will be paid for and how it will get adopted. Right now, the digital health industry is still "coming online" in terms of establishing equitable access for all segments of the socioeconomic spectrum. Digital tech often requires an investment, and not every consumer, employer, or payer is willing to cover the expense associated with using it. But when a specific digital healthcare technology benefits patients, is actively used, improves outcomes, *and also lowers costs* for insurance payers and medical providers, companies and tech pioneers should take notice. I advise companies to prioritize digital health-tech development and implementation because it simply makes good business sense.

> **More specifically, digital tech's ability to offer added healthcare value at a lower cost is what's inducing stakeholders to invest in digital tech and to bring it online.**

Federal Support Is a Big Deal

In fact, the largest payer stakeholder currently investing in the digital healthcare revolution is the US federal government, which funds Medicare. Other agencies are following suit. Consider, for example, that the FDA has also voiced their positive, public-facing stance on digital healthcare:[60]

From mobile medical apps and software that support the clinical decisions doctors make every day to artificial intelligence and machine learning, digital technology has been driving a revolution in healthcare. Digital health tools have the vast potential to improve our ability to accurately diagnose and treat disease and to enhance the delivery of healthcare for the individual.

---

60   "What Is Digital Health?" U.S. Food and Drug Administration, accessed January 2023, https://www.fda.gov/medical-devices/digital-health-center-excellence/what-digital-health.

The use of technologies, such as smartphones, social networks, and internet applications, is not only changing the way we communicate but also providing innovative ways for us to monitor our health and well-being and giving us greater access to information. Together, these advancements are leading to a convergence of people, information, technology, and connectivity to improve healthcare and health outcomes.

The FDA not only endorses its positive take on the advantages conferred by digital healthcare but also clarifies that healthcare stakeholders, including payers, providers, and patients, are using digital health technologies to achieve the following benefits:

- **Reduce inefficiencies**
- **Improve access**
- **Reduce costs**
- **Increase quality**
- **Provide more personalized medicine**

The US agency is so invested in promoting the digital health transformation that it's created a new public health informatics and technology program, the Digital Health Center of Excellence (DHCoE). This agency reiterates the government's commitment to advance digital health, asserting, "Its creation marks the beginning of a comprehensive approach to digital health technology, to advance and realize its full potential."[61]

The agency's objective is to "empower stakeholders to advance healthcare by fostering responsible and high-quality digital health innovation." If you're a company or tech pioneer involved with digital healthcare, this indicates the federal government could partner with

---

61   Ibid.

you. Likewise, the agency is willing to "innovate regulatory approaches to provide efficient and least burdensome oversight."[62] That suggests they're going to cut the regulatory red tape to make it easier for pioneers and providers to develop or implement digital healthcare.

What kind of "less burdensome oversight" is the federal agency referring to? In the case of telemedicine, for example, the website *Women's Health Policy* reports[63] that changing aspects of telehealth policy, coverage, and implementation make telemedicine more accessible. In the Medicare program, that means loosening telehealth restrictions to allow beneficiaries from any geographic location to access services from their homes.

At the state level, the expansion of telehealth in Medicaid programs has been encouraged by relaxing restrictions for provider licensing, online prescribing, and written consent. Many states have also mandated that fully insured private plans must cover and reimburse for telemedicine services just as they would for in-person care (service parity and payment parity). The resulting uptick in telehealth use and availability is clearly a result of these policies. So is the fact that telehealth is saving providers time and money.

Digital Data Transmission

Earlier, I described how smartphone-based pacemaker devices like MyCareLink Heart have helped transform healthcare by transmitting data more effectively and efficiently. Recording and delivering digital information from patients' environments in real time don't just benefit patients medically but also lower costs for providers and payers.

---

62   Ibid.

63   Gabriela Weigel et al., "Opportunities and Barriers for Telemedicine in the U.S. during the COVID-19 Emergency and Beyond," Kaiser Family Foundation, May 11, 2020, https://www.kff.org/womens-health-policy/issue-brief/opportunities-and-barriers-for-telemedicine-in-the-u-s-during-the-covid-19-emergency-and-beyond/.

Provider Benefits

Digital tools are significantly increasing healthcare providers' access to patient data, granting a more accurate view of a patient's health status at any given time. When shared with patients, this clearer appraisal of their health condition prompts better cooperation and treatment compliance. The reason is that patients feel like active partners (rather than passive recipients) in the oversight of their care. Having access to their own patient data promotes a greater sense of control over their health status. It also improves the *overall quality* of providers' care and facilitates *better medical outcomes* at a lower cost.

So making medicine more personalized with patients' digital data boosts the quality of patient care as it reduces inefficiencies and costs. To reap the full potential benefit, providers need to focus on how well the patient uses technology. Providers need to assess how well patients comprehend post-procedure checklists, for example, or understand videos explaining the risks and benefits of procedures for informed consent. It's necessary that providers know how to leverage technology if they're to improve communications like translating instructions and sending reminders to caregivers.

Payer Benefits

In the US healthcare industry, payers are all organizations providing healthcare insurance plans, with the largest single payer being CMS. All told, almost 90 million Americans depend on the healthcare insurance benefits provided by Medicare, Medicaid, and the State Children's Health Insurance Program (SCHIP). Together with private payer organizations, these payer groups (public and private) set medical service rates, collect insurance payments from beneficiaries, process claims, and pay the claims billed by providers. Because of the size and magnitude of CMS as a US healthcare payer, the impact of digital tech's cost-saving and efficiency attributes has massive potential.

AMERICAN HEALTHCARE IS UNIQUE

Despite that potential, the US healthcare ecosystem and the way its different stakeholders interact are extremely complex. The way we structure payments for medical procedures and services and disseminate that information to stakeholders is unique to our country. When we go to the grocery store, we know how much things will cost because items have price tags, and we can compare the cost/benefit of products right away. We can assess a consumer product's quality, brand, and cost and then decide on a method of payment before making a purchase.

But buying healthcare is completely different. We usually don't know the costs or if insurers will cover it right away—or at all. We could accidentally get sick and end up in the ER with a bill that we weren't expecting or won't be able to pay. Many people do. These structural issues within the health system, coupled with an increasing burden on the system itself, make this the optimal time for innovation. It's desperately needed. And many of healthcare's 5P stakeholders are looking to innovation as an exciting and promising way to increase access to more affordable health services.

But the unfortunate truth is that healthcare is the slowest industry "out of the gate" to innovate, and the proven value of digital technologies for healthcare is playing catch up on the heels of the banking and media industries. As healthcare continues going digital, two trends are fueling the frenzy:

1. **Existing technologies are finally being more universally implemented.**

2. **Novel innovations are being welcomed by a far more receptive market.**

Change is upon us, and what you do about the ongoing digital transformation of healthcare will shape the future—that of your company and of the patients it ultimately serves. Even as you read this, companies are moving ahead of their slower competitors, eager to maximize the profitability of digital healthcare's predicted potential.

When it comes to digital health-tech innovation, it's a jungle out there. Healthcare stakeholders need to understand the benefits of tech innovation because it's here to stay. Not only that, but it's also going to keep evolving—as will its benefits. Most of us working in healthcare know how the recent, widespread adoption of telemedicine has resulted in better patient outcomes for less cost. But telemedicine is only the tip of the health-tech iceberg. We all watched how the COVID-19 pandemic accelerated its use and how consumers' uptake of affordable health tech, such as mobile apps and wearables, has kept pace. Digital health tech is now a thriving market, but financing innovation requires creating value for all 5P stakeholders and understanding the role of technology in the greater ecosystem.

MY EXECUTIVE TAKEAWAY

Fortunately, the regulatory environment is more favorable to innovators and entrepreneurs interested in starting digital health companies than it has been in the past.

But pioneers should still prioritize the development and implementation of digital health solutions that are proven to improve health outcomes, be actively utilized by consumers, and lower costs for payers and providers. Another factor to consider is that the digital health industry is still lagging in terms of addressing health equity concerns, so there is opportunity for new companies to be thoughtful about how to accomplish this through their offering and prevent access disparities.

Entrepreneurs and tech pioneers should think critically about their solution's competitors, target population, strategy fit, differentiators, and measures of success so that they are prepared to answer questions from interested payers and providers as they conduct cost/benefit analyses on these solutions. How will it integrate with my company's existing technology?

> - What are your competitors doing in the space?
> - Why focus on a particular population?
> - How does this solution fit into my virtual care/caregiver/home health/AI strategy?
> - How will you measure success, and how long will it take to actually do that?
> - How is this option different from other vendors' solutions?

Once you've completed the preceding assessment, you can apply your answers in a smart, actionable manner. It's absolutely crucial that tech pioneers assess the cost/benefit aspects of offering relevant digital technology and realistically evaluate their ability to do so.

5

DATA DYNAMITE

Unearthing the Digital Healthcare Goldmine
through Analytics and Data Digging

*Data and analytics will support a healthcare system in which it's
more profitable to prevent a stroke than treat one. It is no accident
that right now, a whole set of disruptors in value-based care are
using technology and building on the data infrastructure we set
in motion ten years ago to scale value-based models.*[64]

—FARZAD MOSTASHARI, CEO OF ALEDADE

When the startup Medecision was awarded the Google Cloud Healthcare & Life Sciences Customer Award in 2021, it wasn't a surprise to me or others in the health industry. The digital care management company was supplying solutions and services with the Google Cloud Platform (GCP), offering the real-time data processing and prospective analytics healthcare desperately needed. Shifting away from a retrospective data mindset to real-time analysis was a winning strategy. By the time Medecision won the Google award, leading health plans and care delivery organizations were relying on

---

64   Shubham Singhal et al., "The Next Frontier of Care Delivery: Bringing Care Home,"
      McKinsey & Company, November 30, 2022, https://www.mckinsey.com/industries/
      healthcare/our-insights/the-next-frontier-of-care-delivery-in-healthcare.

the startup to supply technical solutions and services supporting 42 million people nationwide.[65]

The adoption of Google Cloud services allowed Medecision to be more agile and continue developing high-quality products while accelerating their speed to market. Through this collaboration, Medecision leveraged Google Cloud to help its customers recognize and address gaps in patient care by enabling real-time data integration, predictive analytics, and flexible cataloging. Google Cloud also helped Medecision provide real-time visibility to streamline customer experience while also laying the groundwork for more personalized product and feature development. Cloud computing has made all that possible by remotely receiving, storing, and then analyzing big data sets to provide a *nearly endless* array of digital services.

The data mining and analytics that drives cloud computing is also driving the ongoing consolidation of healthcare itself. For health-tech pioneers, that means they'll be selling their digital health solutions to increasingly larger organizations—or partnering with them as Medecision did with Google. Of course, Amazon and Microsoft are looking for those partners too as competition between big tech grows ever more fierce. While the tech giants develop new health tech "in-house," they'll also want to partner with startups to complete their saleable menus of products and services as rapidly as possible. If that sounds like an industry turf war, it *is*.

When I hear some in the health industry refer to Amazon Web Services (AWS) as "one cloud to rule them all," I know they're exaggerating to make a point. But the truth is that a more universal cloud-based care management is a good thing—optimizing healthcare delivery to meet the objectives of VBC: efficiency, effectiveness, and cost reduction.

---

65 "Medecision Wins Google Cloud Healthcare & Life Sciences 2021 Customer Award," Medecision, April 7, 2022, https://blog.medecision.com/google-cloud-award-2021/.

Instead of relying on EHRs and older analytics systems, cloud-based services create more efficient workflow capabilities. These improvements reduce provider-response delays, so quality patient care can be delivered at the correct time using a variety of communication channels.

THE COMPETITION: CLOUD COMPUTING COMPANIES AND SERVICES

It's not just the GCP that's ramping up the development and delivery of innovation but also the other two big cloud service providers too: AWS and Microsoft Azure. Together, they take up 66 percent of the cloud infrastructure market *worldwide*—this increase represents explosive growth, up from 63 percent the previous year.[66] Like Amazon's AWS and Microsoft's Azure, Google's cloud-based platform GCP has helped drive healthcare's continuing trend toward consolidation via integrated delivery networks (IDNs).

IDN Systems Are the Future of Health Delivery

They're a type of ACO, and as such, they constitute a big part of CMS's VBC efforts. IDNs, like ACOs, offer a full range of preventive and acute care services in a certain geographic area. Both are networks of healthcare providers and facilities meant to coordinate and improve the quality of patient care while controlling costs. And they both have hospitals, clinics, and primary care physicians and specialists offering general acute care (as inpatient services) as well as home health services. But what sets IDNs apart from ACOs is that they are a much tighter, more cohesive collection of individual providers and payers, they can

---

66 "Top Cloud Service Providers," CloudZero, accessed January 2023, https://www.cloudzero.com/blog/cloud-service-providers.

sell health insurance plans, and they can also sell health tech directly to group purchasing organizations (GPOs).

Selling Health Tech Requires Data

It's a complicated process to sell digital health tech into the healthcare space, particularly when targeting IDNs and GPOs. Doing so requires some understanding of IDNs and GPOs. And having the right data is going to be key to attracting payers' interests across the healthcare system. What kind of data? I'm referring to the kind that demonstrates pioneers know and understand how to improve clinical and quality metrics of individual care centers. This allows pioneers to customize solutions based on the unique challenges care centers face. Selling directly to IDNs or GPOs will also require familiarity with a facility's specific data because a solution that works for a physician group or urgent care clinic may not work for an acute care hospital.

Pioneers may only have a few products or services to sell, but healthcare facilities, hospitals, clinics, surgery centers, nursing homes, and home health agencies will have hundreds they need to buy. They don't have time to purchase drugs, devices, and other medical products or services, so they use GPO companies to do it for them. These companies oversee all the buying for healthcare providers by collaborating and negotiating with manufacturers on their behalf.

The cost savings they generate for healthcare facilities (including hospitals and nursing homes) are passed onto patients—and ultimately to taxpayers. The fact that they have tens of thousands of product options to choose from gives GPOs strong negotiating clout to make efficient purchasing decisions. As such, a GPO may act as a strong advocate for health-tech pioneers by negotiating a contracted price they can offer to the many payers and providers who rely on their judgment.

HEALTHCARE ECOSYSTEM

COVID-19 is amplifying industry forces diving virtual/digital care in the U.S.

Investors are excited and healthcare incumbents adapt business models

- Investors and established healthcare organizations are making substantial DnA investments
- Embrace of digital care by incumbents (e.g., payors)

Consumer drive demand

- Pressures for innovation and personalization continue to strengthen
- Abrupt shift of care delivery to virtual channels due to COVID-19 fears

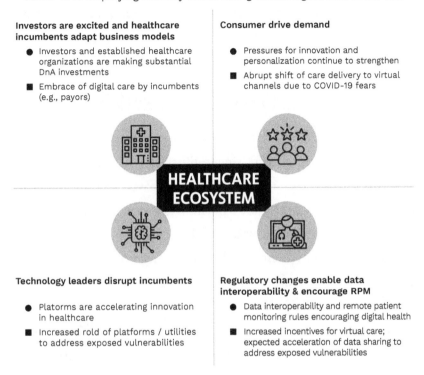

HEALTHCARE ECOSYSTEM

Technology leaders disrupt incumbents

- Platorms are accelerating innovation in healthcare
- Increased rold of platforms / utilities to address exposed vulnerabilities

Regulatory changes enable data interoperability & encourage RPM

- Data interoperability and remote patient monitoring rules encouraging digital health
- Increased incentives for virtual care; expected acceleration of data sharing to address exposed vulnerabilities

● 2019 state of play　■ COVID-19 impact

Source: Shubham Singhal et al., "The Next Wave of Healthcare Innovation: The Evolution of Ecosystems," mckinsey.com, June 23, 2020, https://www.mckinsey.com/industries/healthcare/our-insights/the-next-wave-of-healthcare-innovation-the-evolution-of-ecosystems.

Healthcare Ecosystem: The healthcare ecosystem has changed because of COVID-19, and it's necessary to understand the impact of that change on innovation.

IDNs are expanding as additional providers are being added and as smaller, preexisting IDNs are merging. One example of this consolidation trend is the merger of Atrium Health and Advocate Aurora Health into a $27 billion system in 2022. It created a sixty-seven-hospital system across two distinct geographic areas in the Southeast and Upper Midwest. I tell stakeholders they can expect the merger and acquisition (M&A) activity trend to accelerate. As hospital systems merge and IDNs get larger, they're furthering VBC goals and helping the health industry become less fragmented. Overall, the result is a more affordable health system that consists of streamlined IDN entities using cloud systems to identify where improvements are needed so that strategic decisions can be made.

How IDNs Impact Medical Loss Ratios

The reason IDN savings are so important is because curbing health-care costs is becoming increasingly difficult. These rising costs have put a financial squeeze on medical insurance payers who are concerned about how the new healthcare legislation is impacting their *MLRs*. As I explained in a previous chapter, MLRs define how the total amount of medical insurance premiums they collect from patient/consumers is divided by a payer's costs—with costs being the sum of their medical care expenses plus their administrative costs. If a payer's MLR is adjusted too high in favor of medical care, insurance providers will incur greater losses as they cover more of the administrative costs themselves.

> **Ultimately, payers need to reduce costs and use startup companies to keep their MLRs low.**

The fact that cloud services can reduce these costs is helping payers and providers transition to the value-based medicine model. Another benefit of cloud-based administration is the way its automation tracks the data needed to evaluate and improve an IDN or ACO's performance. It also provides transparency showing how the revenue they get from their premium payments is allocated.

The good news is that being able to expend less time, money, and resources to meet VBC reporting requirements will help reduce ACO, IDN, and payers' MLRs across the entire healthcare system.

CLOUD-BASED POPULATION HEALTH MANAGEMENT

As providers and payers switch over to the VBC approach, it's fueling a growing demand for population health management solutions. Instead of considering the health of one person at a time, both VBC and population health seek to improve the health status and outcomes of groups of people in certain geographic regions. Big tech and their IDN partners (like Medecision) have demonstrated they can apply advanced analytics and data management techniques to improve the poor health of large patient groups at risk of developing chronic disease. When used proactively, these techniques can help ward off diabetes, vascular disease, chronic obstructive pulmonary disease (COPD), hypertension, heart failure, and coronary disease.

> **If something can be measured, it will be measured because the data generated is incredibly useful. So the use of digital analytics will continue to grow as many more applications are discovered and developed by tech pioneers.**

Using this kind of data analytics for population health management helps systems identify populations in need, determine their risk, and track patient progress. This is why many value-based alternate payment plans rely on data ops, multi-model databases, and AI/machine learning tools, data mining, and analytics to assess payer and provider performance. These digital tech tools examine and analyze patient data by grouping patient characteristics. Such analytics can improve patient health outcomes and lower healthcare costs as a result of its ability to examine and track key indicators for patients with chronic diseases. Since these are the patients who usually incur the greatest cost in a practice, that's high-value data. Manual data collection methods can offer benefits too, but it's clear that the demand and adoption of cloud-based products and services will continue to eclipse it as big data and analytics become ubiquitous throughout the health industry.

ANALYTICS IS THE LANGUAGE OF DIGITAL HEALTHCARE

Analytics are needed to organize, graph, monitor, and investigate any marked and unexpected changes in the ocean of digital data healthcare payers and providers must deal with to meet their objectives. Each of these tasks requires the use of statistics, either at a simple level for spotting trends or at an advanced level to see if there's statistical proof of real and significant changes. In the case of healthcare providers, those changes will be used to show an individual medical practice is either moving toward or away from delivering better care to patients. If the collected data shows providers are meeting metrics established by CMS, they'll receive a financial bonus—or face a penalty when they don't. That being the case, it's no surprise some providers aren't happy about the newer VBC system or the scrutiny and constraints it subjects them to. But it's a fact of life in the digitalization of the healthcare industry overall. Savvy use of data analytics and information technology is a good way to orchestrate the complexities of payer-provider relationships in VBC arrangements.

DIGITAL TOOLS FOR VALUE-BASED CARE

Since the digital transformation of the healthcare industry has forced providers and payers to deal with such huge amounts of data, many organizations are opting to use analytical tools that "explain" the significance of this data. This is accomplished through *data mining*, which refers to the exploration and analysis of large information sets (also defined as "big data") to identify meaningful trends and patterns. The automation of current data mining is better for the conventions of statistical analysis. As dependence on manual data entry declines, risk of human error from manually inputting data decreases too. That means data mining not only produces larger amounts of data but that the data itself is more reliable.

The Data Mining and Analytics Sequence

1. *Exploration of data*
2. *Preparation of meaningful analysis*
3. *Modeling of data*
4. *Evaluation through automated systems*
5. *Definition of problem areas*
6. *Future outcome analysis*
7. *Deployment of segregated data*

Data mining is proving helpful in the diagnosis and suggested treatment of illness because of its rapid ability to identify associated symptoms and determine the best course of treatment. These automated capabilities are correcting inequalities within the current healthcare system and increasing its efficiency by reducing the need for manual intervention. In other words, data mining and big data improve *predictive* analytics. Use of data mining is helping reinvent healthcare by alerting providers to situations requiring their involvement and/or intervention.

Closer scrutiny is required, for example, when certain patients are getting readmitted to the hospital too frequently. Fortunately, data mining has demonstrated the ability to accurately predict the likelihood of readmissions so that primary doctors can swing into action and monitor people who might be going back to the hospital too often. Using this approach, the health system can cut costs while improving the health status of the patients they're serving. Sometimes older patients simply forget to take their medicine or haven't gotten a medical test their primary care physician requested. That's a common problem. But if the problem actually involves fraud, data mining can help prevent it in ways that weren't possible before the era of digital health tech.

Predictive Analysis for Reimbursement Cuts

Predictive analysis tools can go a long way toward ensuring patient claims are handled efficiently. This can prevent provider reimbursement cuts, help control costs, and reduce expenses for both payers and providers. Any questionable, unauthorized, or additional claims' expenses can be caught through the AI-enhanced versions of data analytics tools. In addition, medical billing and coding companies can expect to experience a noticeable increase in the value of their operations when they mine their data by using evidence gained from predictive analysis. Its predictive aspect can spur coding companies to adopt strategies developed from the data mining's intelligent evaluations. When implemented, these strategies will increase the likelihood of greater productivity and growth in a company's overall performance. It allows medical coders and billers to incorporate strong and efficient categories into their practice.

Prescriptive Analysis for Rectification

After analysis is undertaken through data mining, the next order of business is a *prescriptive* analysis of the data—an analysis of what needs to be done about the predictions that have been made. Anyone who's invested in the stock market is aware that knowing the market's movement in advance will be very lucrative. Prescriptive analysis of big data offers the potential for huge economic benefit for the healthcare industry as well. An efficiently deployed predictive analytics platform can track the current and upcoming trends, gauge its effect on cash flow, and offer solutions for rectification. For example, if a company is reimbursing claims at a higher or lower level than required, predictive analysis catches the lapse, displays the inefficacies, and offers remedial action through complex algorithms.[67]

Advantages for Medical Billing and Coding

Of course, all the 5P stakeholders are interested in the different takeaways gleaned from data mining and analytics. One of the most relevant use cases for data mining is the automation of medical coding and billing practices that are so central to the industry. For providers, that means they can now outsource their billing and coding service to data companies who can fulfill everything related to that company's services, including their IT infrastructure. And the outsourcing companies themselves can turn around and do the same.

> **In VBC arrangements, data analytics and IT strengthen payer and provider relationships.**

In the case of payers, they no longer need to rely on unwieldy manual audits and complicated procedures to identify misdoing and malpractices among providers. This is why data mining and data analytics are needed to ramp up the automation, precision, and efficiency of the existing billing and coding process. Doing so not only

---

67   Riken Shah, "How the Use of Data Analytics Is Becoming an Authority in Medical Billing Industry," Osplabs, July 26, 2023, https://www.osplabs.com/insights/data-mining-in-medical-coding-and-billing/.

means less fraud and lower payer costs, but it's also a crucial stepping stone in the changeover to a value-based healthcare system.

How Big Data Improves the Medical Billing and Coding Process

- *Cleaner systems of operation with data segregated systematically*
- *Greater transparency from healthcare providers*
- *Reduced costs of manual audits*
- *Lower expenses investigating wrongdoing*
- *Mitigation of malpractice risk*
- *Prediction of patterns and outcomes that increase efficiency*
- *Prevention of waste, fraud, and abuse*

As more providers and payers rely on data mining for their medical billing and coding purposes, it's important to remember these techniques will keep updating into better versions of the original application they spun off from. That means healthcare stakeholders will have to stay current with technical "updates" just like the rest of the IT world if they hope to realize all of digital health tech's potential.

Identifying Fraud

With ongoing instances of fraud in medical billing and coding continually rising, data mining is now being successfully recruited to address and identify fraudulent claims and to eliminate expensive security blunders. Whether it's a fake claim or one that's simply inaccurate, fraud and error have cost the healthcare industry dearly over the years. The National Health Care Anti-Fraud Association conservatively estimates that about 3 percent of our healthcare spending (approximately \$300 billion) is lost to fraud yearly.[68] But those shocking numbers will be declining thanks to the intelligent analytics capability of data mining. This healthcare tech not only identifies fraud but also fosters ways to completely eradicate the possibility of it happening in the first place.

To prevent fraud, data mining technology is used to gather the data from a designated source and then convert it into meaningful analogies and standard measurements within the analytics system. This ultimately culminates in the formation of an enterprise data warehouse (EDW). This EDW works, in turn, as a template against which other data submissions can be compared to identify fraud. Through the EDW, data mining identifies healthcare providers whose coding and billing strategies/actions diverge from predicted norms:

- **Vary from their regular practices**
- **Differ significantly from their competitors**
- **Deviate from the normal process**

After identifying which providers show these deviations, that selected group is examined further to gather more information using the following identifiers:

- **Area of practice**
- **Location**
- **Type of healthcare service offered**
- **Frequency of billing**
- **Size of operations**

---

68   Nishamathi Kumaraswamy et al, "Healthcare Fraud Data Mining Methods: A Look Back and Look Ahead," National Center for Biotechnology Information, October 19, 2021, https://www.ncbi.nlm.nih.gov/pmc/articles/PMC9013219/.

By using both sets of EDW data to conduct healthcare data analytics, fraudsters can be identified and stopped. Although it's a form of scrutiny not everyone appreciates, it does serve the intended purpose of saving money by eliminating fraud and inefficiencies. Doing so creates the more value-based healthcare model US policymakers have legislated.

DATA MINING ADOPTION CHALLENGES

While it's clear that data mining and predictive analytics offer exciting benefits to the medical billing and coding industry, many industry professionals have yet to adopt these techniques. Part of the reason is confusion among industry professionals about the exact nature of data mining's capabilities and advantages. Their hesitancy also stems from an attachment to conventional audit and compliance methods, which are undertaken through mostly manual statistical collection. Some providers are concerned, for example, that relying exclusively on automated systems may subject them to audits and unnecessary investigations that aren't justified.

Data Mining Implementation Challenges

- Uncertainty of predictive data mining results that may not occur
- Reliance on technological statistics as opposed to manual operations
- Cost of data-generated audits that weren't justified
- Jobs lost from technology replacing the manual generation of statistics
- Ignorance of data mining's benefits in the healthcare industry

Despite these understandable concerns, the benefits of data mining techniques for providers far outweigh the challenges implicit to its adoption and implementation. In fact, using big data, data mining, and data analytics is vital to the digital healthcare revolution as a whole. And the reality is that most payer stakeholders already rely on big data to ensure their medical billing and coding are optimally efficient and accurate.

As data mining and analytics continue to evolve and become more effective, payer and provider stakeholders will feel increasing pressure to adopt them and work together. Those who don't will struggle to meet policymakers' value-based model performance objectives and are likely to face financial penalties.

BIG DATA IS EVOLVING—SO WHAT'S NEXT?

Most digital health pioneers already understand that data-driven analytics and the machine learning aspect of AI are essential to the success of the VBC approach and alternative payment models. Together, these leading-edge digital health tools measure the provider performance and patient outcomes so foundational to the VBC approach that policymakers have mandated to improve healthcare's quality and efficiency. And this takeaway's true whether analytics and AI are being used in the context of fee-for-service reimbursement, total-cost-of-care models, or other alternative payment approaches.

Digital health tech's RPM and telemedicine capabilities, as well as the increasing use of big data, blockchain, and AI, are all changing the face of healthcare. These technologies are driving the success of VBC and the alternative payment models that fund them. It's definitely in the best interest of healthcare stakeholders to "upgrade." And by that, I mean the 5P stakeholders need to use health-tech solutions that support VBC and alternative payment models.

The potential for *blockchain* in healthcare, for instance, relates to its ability to conceptualize and distribute trust across networks. A type of shared database, blockchain stores different types of information as data in blocks that are linked together via cryptography. Blockchain technology utilizes decentralized networks, in which each member of the network has access to the same information. This dissuades parties from exerting influence or authority over one another in a way that negatively impacts the network's functionality, while it also helps optimize resource distribution.

In the context of healthcare, blockchain has transformative applications, including facilitating secure transfer and protection of patient data, supporting healthcare data interoperability (the ability of healthcare IT systems and software to communicate and exchange data), and enabling real-time tracking of and access to patient data. I predict growing adoption of blockchain by ACOs because of the lack of ACO-specific software and legacy applications that can sufficiently accomplish these functions.

Problems Solved by Blockchain in Provider/Payer Networks

- *Claims clearing*
- *Provider directory*
- *Patient directories*
- *Master patient index*
- *Provider credentialing*

As a digital healthcare analyst who follows technology trends, I want to stress the importance of decision-makers, innovators, developers, and entrepreneurs knowing which tech to offer payers who are using alternate payment models. Being able to deliver the tech they want and need is key. CMS itself is encouraging payers and providers to embrace specific digital tech that provides better value for reduced cost. Wearable devices that allow patients/providers to monitor a patient's health status are just one example of digital tools that lower healthcare costs while improving patient outcomes. In this particular example, providers are able to access patients' health data in ways they can leverage to improve that patient's health. That's the endgame, after all—to deliver better healthcare value to patients.

MY EXECUTIVE TAKEAWAY

Data analytics allows providers to gain insights from performance management measures and metrics. And it's those assessments that enable financial viability under risk-based and pay-for-performance contracts. That being the case, it's important to remember these big data techniques are just one part of an entire constellation of digital healthcare technologies. As such, it's exciting that data mining and its resulting analytics are continuing to benefit the healthcare industry in unprecedented ways:

- ➢ Help healthcare stakeholders understand how new healthcare legislation and payment reforms will impact their bottom line
- ➢ Are useful in helping payers keep their MLRs down in the face of rising healthcare costs
- ➢ Can identify high-risk populations and target interventions to address their complex health needs
- ➢ Enable effective predictive patient analysis by identifying diagnoses and treatments based on patient characteristics and points of provider intervention to prevent further patient deterioration and higher healthcare costs incurred by readmissions or disease complications

➢ Support the detection and prevention of fraudulent activity, efficiently point out medical billing and coding errors, and prompt investigations to correct and minimize their disrupted efficiency and effectiveness

Thanks to the predictive ability of data analysis, the healthcare industry now has the technical means to operate more efficiently. AI-driven data mining and analytics will continue to facilitate lower health-delivery costs and the better quality and outcomes needed for the success of VBC and alternative payment models. Just as important, I'll share key knowledge you need to know about payer contracting arrangements in the chapter ahead.

PAYER CONTRACTING ARRANGEMENTS

Meeting Payer Goals Drives Innovation

We are creating and delivering innovative, data-driven solutions to help improve consumers' lives and the communities we serve.

—ASHOK CHENNURU, GLOBAL CHIEF DATA AND INSIGHTS OFFICER, ELEVANCE

The world of payer contracting arrangements is complex, spanning federal regulations, reimbursement models, and financial incentives. Before we dive into the weeds of those details, let's first examine three key questions to consider as you set out to meet payer goals:

1. *What motivates payers?* Payers have their own competing priorities to balance, namely, maximizing ROI, providing member benefits, and optimizing MLRs (more on this later). Understanding payer motivation is crucial.

2. *How do payers get reimbursed?* There's a maze of possible reimbursement mechanisms—fee-for-service, value-based contracts, and more. We'll map out some of the most common methods of reimbursement later in this chapter.

3. *How is technology paid for?* Innovators need to know not just what payers want but also how to get their products covered

and reimbursed. We'll walk through some reimbursement strategies and contracting frameworks.

With that high-level understanding of payer motivations, reimbursement models, and technology funding pathways, let's explore payer arrangements further.

UNDERSTANDING THE PAYER

Among healthcare's 5P stakeholders, the payer space is the most complicated by far. If you're a pioneer marketing innovation, that means coming to grips with the complexity of how payers get reimbursed and planning benefit for their bottom line as well as your own. Spoiler alert: that's not easy! In fact, some in the health industry have compared trying to comprehend payer contracting arrangements to studying *quantum physics*. I'd say that's pretty accurate. But it's not optional. You'll have to figure out the gist of payer reimbursement strategies—either on your own or with the help of industry advisers. Understanding those arrangements and how they can be used to benefit payers is the only way to successfully sell your health tech.

A good starting place for pioneers who are trying to sell their tech to an insurance company payer is asking yourself why an insurance company would want you as a vendor. It's because you either reduce their medical costs, so that it's a cost savings, or it increases their revenue because it's improving membership.

So getting your foot in the door and showing a payer they need your digital tech is just your first step. The second one is figuring out how a payer will be able to pay for your digital tech in a way that's profitable for *their* ROI. That's because proving *benefit* in addition to profitability is the main priority for the nine hundred health insurance companies/payers in the US offering commercial and private (employer) health coverage. One big reason is that the public payer, CMS, is using its federal clout to implement the cost/benefit goals of VBC throughout the health industry. In its role as public payer, CMS uses taxpayer dollars to fund 34.4 percent of healthcare, while the remaining 67.3 percent is funded by commercial or private, for-profit corporations.

If a payer adopts a device that monitors blood sugar for diabetics, for example, and those patients are able to reduce their *high A1C marker* from thirteen to eleven, it's obviously good for the patient. Having a high A1C marker indicates difficulty regulating glucose levels, and an A1C of 6.5 percent or higher indicates diabetes. Any A1C over 9 percent is considered dangerous, leading to complications like blindness, nerve damage, and kidney failure.[69] So the blood sugar monitoring device would fill an important medical need. But if the tech costs $1,000 per patient, and it doesn't yield fewer hospitalizations and fewer doctor visits over twelve months, then it won't result in a good ROI. It doesn't enable the company to make the $1,000 back within those twelve months. So it doesn't make sense as an investment, unless it qualifies for other areas such as Stars measures or HEDIS measures that are a requirement for payers to meet certain healthcare quality metrics as mentioned in early chapters.

How well a health-tech pioneer understands a payer's mindset and needs will inevitably dictate a payer's decision to select or reject a pioneer's health tech. Payer realities will shape their purchasing decisions, and watching/responding to those purchasing trends allows

---

69   "Managing Blood Sugar: Hemoglobin A1C (HbA1C) Test," Centers for Disease Control and Prevention, August 11, 2022, https://www.cdc.gov/diabetes/managing/managing-blood-sugar/a1c.html.

pioneers to align their sales tactics. Understanding *why* another startup's approach is working and *how to modify or replicate it* for your own tech and a payer's set of industry constraints is crucial to pioneers' success.

PIONEERS NEED A PAYER MINDSET

Smart tech pioneers, a.k.a. *vendors* or *contractors*, will identify what marketing approach has already succeeded with payers and then do likewise. Just as pioneers need to understand what's working (and what isn't) in the technical and business areas of tech development, they need to do the same for the payers that they're selling to. As pioneers emulate what's working, they'll modify their business case to suit the payers' needs. To spell that out, I mean pioneers must step into a payer's shoes and comprehend their world: compete with other payers (those nine hundred other insurers) and identify what payer business strategies are winning in the *current* set of market conditions.

As of 2023, the following insurance companies were the top five private insurance payers:[70]

1. *UnitedHealth Group: 51 million members*
2. *Elevance Health (formerly Anthem): 47.5 million members*
3. *Centene: 27 million members*
4. *Aetna (merged with CVS): 24.4 million members*
5. *Cigna: 18 million members*

Established health-tech companies and startups both need to be competing to create value for payers. They can do that by offering

---

70 "Top 5 Largest Health Insurance Payers in the United States," Health Payer Intelligence, August 28, 2023, https://healthpayerintelligence.com/news/top-5-largest-health-insurance-payers-in-the-united-states.

payers digital health-tech solutions that not only fill gaps in health-care delivery and management but also increase payers' ROI over a twelve-month period.

WHAT PAYERS WANT

If you don't understand the revenue build for your own tech-sales pipeline and a payer's too, you won't be able to build a health-tech business. Both are absolutely essential to navigate the complex cross-currents of payer priorities. No matter how needed and useful your tech innovation may be to some aspect of healthcare, payer business realities will loom larger. Those payers making the decision to fund (or not fund) digital health tech have to show corporate why adopting it makes sense financially—why it's a smart move based on a company's quarterly returns and to its all-important ROI.

It's difficult for payers to achieve all three of their primary objectives as insurers: *maximize ROI, benefit their members,* and also *balance their company's MLR.* So pioneers selling their health tech to payers need to understand how it will benefit payers in one (or more) of those three areas even if it's great for patients or providers.

A PAYER'S FUNDING FRAMEWORK

Having been part of the payer world myself, I can vouch for the fact that you'll have to unlock the payer space if you want to get the healthcare ecosystem to pay for your digital tech or services. The problem is that the payer space is very complex, so I'm providing the following payer contracting arrangement framework as a starting point.

This chart presents the different billing mechanisms payers can use to reimburse you for your digital health tech. It depicts one mechanism for federal billing and one for direct-to-consumer billing, among many others. For payers funding health tech, it's really a process of cherry-picking or mixing and matching appropriate, strategic combinations of the billing mechanisms available to them. So like it or not, it's up to a pioneer selling their tech to channel the payer mindset and identify the multiple funding opportunities a payer has access to.

	CONTRACT TYPE	LINES OF BUSINESS	BILLING MECHANISM	
VENDOR (TRADITIONAL OR RESELLER)	MSA SOW SaaS	Medicare Medicaid Commercial	Invoice	Per member per month / Per engaged member / milestones/ utilization
		Commercial Only	Claims-based billing	case rate / milestones
VENDOR (DIRECT TO CLIENT)	Direct contract	Commercial self-funded only	Invoice to client	Depends on integration
	BAA, DUA, etc.		Claims	$30K clients per payer to set up data exchange
PROVIDER	Fee schedule	Medicare Medicaid Commercial	Standard claims submission	Utilization (fee-based) or case rate depending on payer and need being filled
PROVIDER & VENDOR	Vendor – MSA & provider fee schedule	Medicare Medicaid Commercial	Depends on arrangement	Can do both pmpm and fee schedule or just case rate through claims

Payer Contracting Arrangement Framework: Direct-to-consumer companies need to know how to help payers transition to digital health reimbursement arrangements.

Although this payer contracting framework only represents a fraction of the knowledge base I've acquired working with payers, it's helpful as a starting point for tech pioneers. It's useful for setting strategy (when customized) to meet specific corporate objectives and requirements. So to help you conceptualize the payer mindset more clearly, I'll explain a sampling of the basic reimbursement factors to consider when mixing different aspects of payer contracting arrangements.

ROI Reimbursement Strategies

Such help is key because the ROI strategy for selling tech to a *commercial* payer versus an *employer* payer is going to be different. When you sell your tech to a *commercial payer*, you'll have to prove how that tech will add to their ROI within a *twelve-month period*. By way of contrast, an *employer payer* has the longer runway of three years to prove the ROI for your tech's impact.

Payers' Twelve-Month ROI Window

Why are twelve months used to measure ROI for commercial insurers? Because payers' members frequently shift from one insurance carrier to another, and they do it in twelve-month cycles during annual reenrollment periods—especially when they're enrolled in Medicare Advantage plans provided by commercial insurance companies. So a payer company will only invest in health tech if it addresses two things: (1) a really common health problem that new enrollees require or want and (2) one that lowers doctor visits, ER visits, or hospitalizations.

Tech pioneers need to put on their payer "spectacles" and view new digital health tech through the lens of a payer's ROI. Nonsurgical cancer detection with liquid biopsy is another apt example of innovation that payers might question from a twelve-month ROI perspective (more on this in the final chapter). Yes, patients will love that liquid biopsy is a noninvasive cancer test, but its relatively infrequent use among a payer's membership, combined with a single-use cost of $800–900 per test, won't make it a good tech investment for a payer.

Why would I pay for that if the risk of cancer is statistically quite low? They'll ask. Even if liquid biopsy caught 0.1 percent of cancers, it wouldn't necessarily reduce the cost of treatment for a payer unless the cancers were caught very early. So again, it's hard for a payer to justify from the ROI perspective.

On the flip side, it's likely a payer *would* approve a digital solution for a fertility app that kept track of a pregnant woman and made sure she stayed safe and healthy. Such apps help women catch early issues, prevent preterm births, and have a natural vaginal birth as opposed to a C-section. For payers, the cost of a natural birth averages about $15,000 versus $26,000 for a C-section.[71] Saving more than $10,000 per member is an outcome that could significantly and routinely reduce payer costs over the relatively short (less than twelve-month) period of a woman's pregnancy. Helping a member avoid preterm birth and the expense of a neonatal nursery increases those savings too. Optimally, it's those two factors: the short-term cost-of-care savings provided by new tech *plus* its ability to attract new members, which will influence a payer's decision to adopt it or reject it.

Even if a health plan doesn't pay for a pioneer's tech or service, there's still opportunity within a commercial line of business to make it happen as long as they get the funding right. In the case of a traditional vendor, this could be software as a service, or it could be a hormone test sold direct to the consumer. And you could still function as a vendor and contract with a commercial payer at the same time. In other words, *you can offer your tech to different clients simultaneously.* Instead of putting all your eggs in one basket, this approach protects you from any one client going under or opting out. And you can do all of this under a traditional vendor arrangement. So if you're a pioneer/vendor, it adds to your versatility because you can offer different payment options.

---

71 Elizabeth Rivelli, "How Much Does It Cost to Have a Baby?" Forbes Advisor, accessed January 2023, https://www.forbes.com/advisor/health-insurance/average-childbirth-cost/.

Simplify Contracting So That Payers Spend Less

Digital tech pioneers have to document the value of their tech or service to a payer's bottom line. While the tech obviously has to provide value to patients and healthcare systems, it also has to prove a real financial ROI in both the short and long term. One way to do that is being able to address multiple care modalities through a single vendor, a method that is extremely attractive to payers. Since payer funding is what's driving most healthcare innovation, it's crucial for pioneers to have a basic understanding of payer priorities and payer contracting arrangements.

From a payer's point of view, managing fewer vendors who offer more product and service value also means greater economy resulting from less per-item cost negotiations. These two reasons explain why payers prefer vendors that can provide more than one service or product and prefer those that can meet a range of needs rather than just a single-point solution. Dealing with one vendor who offers multiple solutions helps payers streamline their evaluation and purchasing processes, and it also offers the potential to meet a range of comorbidities affecting individual members. And there's also tremendous value in being able to offer flexible products and services that payers can use to "triage" individual members' care up or down as needed. Digital tech that's versatile, flexible, and widely applicable offers significant value to payers as they seek to streamline their systems.

Payers Love PMPM Contracting

One contracting arrangement that's attractive to both payers and pioneer/vendors is the *per-member-per-month (PMPM) approach*. In this arrangement, payers don't have to worry about utilization rates or how seasonality effects use of a digital health product or service. And widespread applicability among a large number of members means payers can fund tech for 0.50 cents or even 0.02 cents per month per person as opposed to $500 per person. That higher cost occurs as tech use targets more specific populations. So a payer won't want to pay PMPM for more exclusive tech that few people actually use.

Still, PMPM is the preferred way for health plans to sell services to employer plans because it's revenue they can count on without having to prove it. Payers know what their accounting books are going to look like because there's no variation (and no financials that can't be accurately forecast). Charging 0.02 cents for five hundred members creates an easy calculation. Fortunately, the PMPM contracts help digital health startups scale, because they can anticipate their return based on the known number of members using it. So startup vendors love this approach. But brokers/consultants hate it, because they know a certain number of members aren't using the tech or service, and they deem that wasteful.

However, if you do PMPM on the plan side, you can vary the cost. And what that means is everyone gets a bill at the end of every month, and that bill might say administrative costs, medical expense, or something else. So by doing PMPM as a plan expense, the plan can choose to bury the new tech expense under their admin expense. So everyone's admin expense for the plan goes up a bit, but nobody really knows why it went up.

Folding the cost of new tech into admin expense for an insurance plan is useful because employers or individual members won't get riled up over bearing the expense for tech they don't need. A company without many women won't want to see a line item for maternity nor will members over childbearing age. But if it's there (hidden in administrative costs) and not used, it's considered revenue for both the payer and the pioneer. Payers make a lot of money on things people don't use. So it's smart for plans to do this even though consultants and brokers hate it.

Again, payer plan administrators prefer it this way because it allows accurate expense/revenue forecasting while permitting the transfer pricing (from expense category to category) I just mentioned. It's far easier to embed the expense across five million members than to try to count accurately every month which of them used what item. And you can also embed things that don't necessarily apply to everyone (like maternity), but because it's so inexpensive, no one's going to complain too much if it's only a two-cent increase per member.

Service-Level Agreement Contracts

As an alternative to the PMPM arrangement that pays a flat fee for every payer member, pioneers/vendors can suggest payers use a service-level agreement (SLA). This type of contract will only reimburse a vendor for the members that actually use their tech. An SLA is an option if their tech is addressing a health need affecting a smaller group and they want to increase their revenue. It's also appropriate for an agreement involving a software as a service (SaaS), a hosting relationship, or some other tech-related service relationship where the customer cares about service delivery standards and metrics and not just about accomplishing a particular service milestone.

That's why an SLA could be a good option in a business relationship with a Health Information Technology (HIT) service, in a backup or disaster-recovery relationship, or in a data-service relationship. In all of these scenarios, a payer might want more data beyond the fact that a particular task was performed. But payers don't like this approach as much because it's harder to forecast how many members will use the tech and how often.

Although SLA contracts are sometimes an appropriate payer option, their overuse can negatively impact payer operations. If tech engagement drops too low because of seasonality or other factors, payers may have to cut staff. PMPM avoids this possibility by providing steady, predictable financials so that a payer can keep their staffing stable. But you can't predict that outcome with SLAs based on member engagement.

EFFECTIVENESS VERSUS EFFICACY: KNOW THE DIFFERENCE

As a pioneer, your top priority is helping payers face their situational challenges in healthcare. Letting your data tell your story is best. But needing to generate data on a clinical model's outcomes *in advance* is tricky prior to winning a payer contract. You can do that by conducting an actuarial analysis using general commercial data (not generated by your solution). When calculating the ROI for your solution, such data can serve as a proxy. Using this approach will allow you to provide data that proves the *effectiveness* rather than the *efficacy* of your tech solution.

What's the difference? *Effectiveness refers to results gained in a clinical or a real-world environment,* whereas *efficacy refers to results acquired under controlled or ideal conditions.* One way to generate effectiveness data on your health tech is by launching your startup as a *direct-to-consumer, cash-pay service.* This way, you can validate both the demand for your solution and its early outcomes. In the final analysis, showing a payer that patients are paying out of pocket for your tech is one of the most powerful payer inducements you can use.

rents were advised to make the eight-hour drive to Children's
al of Philadelphia (CHOP) for a second opinion.

hen Rowan's scans at CHOP showed the cancer nodules in her
ere growing, her oncologists turned to precision medicine and
genetic testing. It turned out she had one of the common can-
ng genetic alterations: a neurotrophic tyrosine receptor kinase
That designation refers to an NTRK gene fusion, which is a
omarker found in over twenty-five different types of cancer. To
t, the TRK-inhibitory medicine, larotrectinib, was prescribed
he tumor, inhibit its growth, and shrink existing nodules.
owan's case, that therapy took two months, and it also meant
another round of radioactive iodine therapy. Since that final
ared her residual cancer so successfully, Rowan was able to
the medicine altogether. Early evidence indicates medica-
arotrectinib prevent the genetic mutations causing certain
ey also increase cancer cell uptake of radioactive iodine to
herapy more effective.

examples of precision medicines include Kymriah and
hese chimeric antigen receptor T-cell therapies were
the FDA for hematologic malignancies. Zolgensma
recision medicine, used in adeno-associated virus gene
pinal muscular atrophy. Even though the current model
ment wasn't configured for these high price-point drugs,
eing addressed with reimbursement policy adjustments
to *individual* outcomes rather than *group* outcomes.
later.

IS GETTING MORE PRECISE

cision Medicine (PGx) like that offered by CHOP
pitals is the most complex and costly application of

MY EXECUTIVE TAKEAWAY

Health-tech pioneers must understand what payers want and need
when selling their tech. In addition to rising costs, pioneers need to
understand the issues payers face and show how their innovations
will help payers cope with the following health industry pain points:

- **Confusion over uncertain healthcare reform**
- **Lack of IT/systems integration and security**
- **Incentives that align with healthcare providers**
- **Better consumer education/understanding of costs and coverage**
- **Consumer education/self-responsibility for health**
- **Increase in patient pay/high-deductible health plans**
- **Providers entering the payer space**
- **Providers in the process of consolidation**
- **Fewer medical professionals for case management**
- **Growth of employer self-insurance**

Besides your internal development team, pioneers will need the
help of an outside advisor to understand the bewildering complexity
of payer reimbursement options when negotiating with a buyer. That
outside advisor needs to be an expert in reimbursement solutions
so that they can suggest the optimal option for a particular payer.
Competition in the digital health-tech market is fierce. So a pioneer
will need to show the technical benefits of their solution for payers as
well as the optimal ways payers can get reimbursed for it. And they
need to be aware that certain tools can be more challenging to bring
to market. Precision medicine is one of them, and I'll explain why in
the chapter ahead.

7

PAYERS PHA
GENE ODY

Unraveling Genomi

*It's time to ask not only what g
can we work on those genes*

—LON CARDI

As a physician with young child
as a new therapeutic tool tha
need arises. Knowing how it help
cancer hits close to home. When
started having trouble swallowin
for months. After visiting differe
nose/throat specialist noticed a

The biopsy he ordered ir
a CT scan showed it was alr
lungs. Since the cancer had s
to remove her thyroid and ly
therapy for her lungs. In R
cally eradicate her cancer, ar

Her p
Hospi
W
lungs w
ordered
cer-driv
fusion.
cancer b
combat i
to target
In R
finishing
round cle
stop takin
tions like
cancers. Th
make that
Other
Yescarta. T
approved b
is another p
therapy for s
of reimburse
this issue is b
that will link
More on that

MEDICIN

Advanced Pre
and other hos

this therapeutic tool. At the other end of the expense spectrum (and much more affordable), at-home genetic testing is being covered by payers and offered to health consumers directly. Blue Cross Blue Shield of Michigan, for instance, has partnered with the precision medicine vendor OneOme to offer at-home genetic testing. They're doing that through the company's nonprofit health maintenance organization (HMO)—Blue Care Network. As of 2022, the network added pharmacogenomics (the study of how genes affect someone's response to drugs) to its array of solutions for its 840,000 members.[72] To make sure physicians give patients the correct medication early in their treatment, the company instituted a Blue Cross Personalized Medicine and pharmacogenomics program. It was a timely and much-needed move, as precision/personalized medicine relies heavily on genomic data.

More payers are realizing they also need to offer their member populations pharmacogenomics to stay competitive. As they do so, they'll need to identify high-quality labs providing clinician-decision support, integrate the pharmacogenomics data into member EHRs, and pair pharmacogenomics testing with chronic disease medication management. Using pharmacogenomic testing will help their providers decide which medications to use and which to avoid. Knowing an individual patient's genetic profile will allow them to better adjust and tailor a patient's medications and dosages. In the end, that outcome will improve payers' ROI as their members' health improves.

---

72   Kelsey Waddill, "Payer Precision Medicine Program Covers At-Home Genetic Tests," HealthPayerIntelligence, accessed January 2023, https://healthpayerintelligence. com/news/payer-precision-medicine-program-covers-at-home-genetic-tests.

FOLLOW THE MONEY INTO PRECISION MEDICINE

Although affordability and access challenges have blocked precision medicine's widespread use in the past, that situation is changing rapidly. The five biggest legacy payers, including UnitedHealth Group, Anthem, Aetna, Cigna, and Humana, are actively involved in efforts to make precision medicine available to providers and patients. They can see it's going to help shape the future of healthcare by avoiding the physical and psychological complications of wrong, less precise treatment. These payers and providers know early detection and treatment are key to ensuring patients' best quality of life. Other stakeholders who "follow the money" understand that legacy payers' increased involvement has hinged on the simultaneous, ongoing development of other digital healthcare technologies. One example is the way an EHR can smoothly integrate pharmacogenomics data into its design.

Now that leading payers are backing precision medicine's implementation, other payer and provider stakeholders are entering the precision medicine arena. Using it most effectively, however, requires providers to know each patient's health habits and to understand their individual genetic, metabolic, and social reality. Tracking those factors may seem challenging, but digital health tech like wearable apps, electronic medical records, and AI are making that doable.

PRECISION MEDICINE TESTS, TOOLS, AND THERAPIES

Operating from a molecular understanding of disease, precision medicine relies on analyzing a vast amount of data derived from different sources: both biological and digital. Those sources include genomes and electronic medical records as well as mobile health devices. Analyzing all those digital data to compare links between a typical genome and variants that might indicate, or lead to, disease used to be an expensive, complicated challenge. And after it was analyzed, it had to be translated into precision diagnostic tests and targeted therapies, using implementation tools that are compatible with the modern healthcare environment. Fortunately, for stakeholders, that whole process has become much less complicated and costly for healthcare payers, providers, and patients.

Precision medicine became a practical tool only relatively recently when the digital technologies of AI and machine learning were deployed in the health sector. AI has been able to convert the torrent of big data gleaned from clinical, genetic, genomic, and environmental information into the smart data precision medicine relies upon.

Being able to parse big data with AI was the missing component needed to make leading-edge genomics research and innovation accessible for diagnostic tests, digital tools, and targeted therapies. For 5P healthcare stakeholders, that means the availability of this "intelligent" data has brought the insights of genomics within reach. Many of these stakeholders already see the clear benefit of optimizing patient care and outcomes with more precise medication management and/or prevention strategies and genomic cancer tests.

An example is the FoundationOne®CDx diagnostic test, which is able to flag mutations in 324 genes and two genomic signatures in solid tumors. The test can also indicate which of the fifteen existing FDA-approved cancer treatments is likely to be most helpful to patients with one of five tumor types, including non-small cell lung cancer, melanoma, breast cancer, colorectal cancer, and ovarian cancer.[73] Cancer is the second leading cause of death in the US (after heart disease). In 2020 alone, there were 602,350 cancer deaths in the US. This kind of genomic diagnostic test can make a huge difference by reducing cancer mortality and the terrible price it enacts from patients, their families, and the US economy.[74]

> **The Agency for Healthcare Research and Quality estimates the direct economic impact of that cancer rate in the US is around $80 billion per year in terms of lost productivity, wages, and caregiver needs that drain billions more from the economy.**[75]

Gene and cell therapies/drugs are also being refined or developed to address diseases associated with defective or missing genes, providing cures for such diseases. Because the two approaches are different, some protocols utilize both *gene therapy* and *cell therapy* in a patient's treatment. In the case of gene therapy, a faulty gene is replaced, or a new one is added in an attempt to cure disease or improve your body's ability to fight diseases, such as cancer, cystic fibrosis, heart disease, diabetes, hemophilia, or AIDS. Cell therapy, on the other hand, is a type of regenerative medicine that involves the direct transfer of cells with the needed function into a patient. Some examples are bone marrow transplantation and FDA-approved stem cell therapies that use umbilical cord blood to treat cancer or immune disorders.

---

73 Jennifer Bresnick, "What Are Precision Medicine and Personalized Medicine?" HealthITAnalytics, May 1, 2020, https://healthitanalytics.com/features/what-are-precision-medicine-and-personalized-medicine.

74 "Update on Cancer Deaths in the United States," Centers for Disease Control and Prevention, accessed January 2023, https://stacks.cdc.gov/view/cdc/119728/cdc_119728_DS1.pdf

75 Jennifer Bresnick, "WWhat Are Precision Medicine and Personalized Medicine?"

> Gene therapy and cell therapy approaches and products have the potential to transform continuous treatment for a debilitating disease into a one-time solution.

Once the proper gene and cell therapy or drug is administered, affected patients would only require follow-ups from a physician to check the therapy's efficacy and safety. Unfortunately, gene therapies currently come with a hefty, multimillion-dollar price tag that creates issues for payers who are unable to accrue this expense as a single payment in their budgets without a negative financial impact. But just as genomic testing costs started high and then dropped to become increasingly affordable, the same trend is expected for the next generation of gene and cell therapies/drugs in the years ahead.

REMOVING ROADBLOCKS FOR PRECISION MEDICINE

A network of health partners has already started interacting to make precision medicine available to patients. These stakeholder/players include *investors, tech pioneers, insurance payers,* and *medical providers* who are actively analyzing the next steps needed to make the benefits of precision medicine widely accessible to the patients who need it. As of 2013, Medicare reported that 1,455,162 fee-for-service beneficiaries had utilized precision medicine in some way, billing for $256,242,345.[76] Most of those patients had opted for pharmacogenomics (also referred to as pharmacogenetics) testing to determine how their genes would affect their response to the drugs being considered for their treatment. That high demand is undoubtedly why CMS

---

76 Umberto Tirelli et al., "Precision Medicine in Oncology: Origins, Applications and New Perspectives," *Genes & Immunity* 22 (February 2021): 103–111. doi: 10.1038/s41435-021-00150-1.

decided to start covering FDA-approved (or cleared) laboratory diagnostic laboratory tests using Next-Generation Sequencing (NGS) for patients with germline (inherited) ovarian or breast cancer in 2020.[77]

RESOLVE BILLING AND DOCUMENTATION HURDLES

Despite high patient demand for precision medicine, problems with traditional billing and documentation are slowing its utilization. Unfortunately, the standardization of billing practices and codes needed for precision medicine testing has lagged far behind the emergence of new genomic tests. As a result, providers often resort to using methodology-based codes rather than gene-specific codes. This practice has allowed laboratories to bill for tests that don't have clinical relevance—a reality that's eroded the economic benefit of precision medicine testing for insurers. Poor documentation of testing claims in EHRs has also made it difficult for stakeholders to determine the effect of precision medicine on patient outcomes. To tackle billing and documentation hurdles, payers are deploying operational teams using exponential computer technologies that allow them to work and operate more efficiently.

Educate and Reassure Consumers

Precision medicine has opened an entirely new market, offering consumer resources and platforms providing better understanding of the complex genomic factors influencing health. The value

---

77 "CMS Expands Coverage for Next Generation Sequencing as a Diagnostic Tool for Patients with Breast and Ovarian Cancer," Centers for Medicare & Medicaid Services, March 16, 2022, https://www.cms.gov/newsroom/press-releases/cms-expands-coverage-next-generation-sequencing-diagnostic-tool-patients-breast-and-ovarian-cancer.

to consumers is huge and still expanding, allowing them access to unprecedented levels of more personalized treatment for a variety of chronic conditions, illnesses, and cancers. Growing consumer interest in precision medicine is having a positive impact, driving more payer and provider involvement.

> **As a first step, payers and providers need to educate consumers/patients on the clinical utility of precision medicine and data protection.**

Consumers won't be aware of precision medicine's benefits unless providers and insurers educate them about the specific ways precision medicine can help them. Part of that educational effort needs to address consumer concerns about the security of any genetic data they submit for testing. And payers offering insurance coverage for at-home genetic testing is another important signal to consumers that health plans are willing to make this financial investment in their health outcomes.

Ensure Provider Capability

During the last decade, providers have had to adjust to healthcare's accelerating digital transformation and the use of big data, AI, machine learning, telehealth, and a host of other newer technologies. It's not surprising providers feel overwhelmed at the prospect of implementing precision medicine and going through yet another tech-adoption process that disrupts their practice protocols. But precision medicine's ability to give providers more targeted testing and treatment options for individual patients makes it well worth it.

To reap the benefits of precision medicine, providers need to acquire a full understanding of its potential for their patients. That benefit is based on its ability to more effectively target medication that's appropriate for each of their patients' unique needs. As a relatively new treatment option, precision medicine's value to patients and consumers largely depends on providers doing three things:

1. Acquire and stay current in any precision medicine training they need

2. Get or expand access to the genomic testing services used in precision medicine

3. Educate patients to instill confidence in provider expertise in precision medicine

The combined use of big data, AI, machine learning, and genomics has finally given providers access to more effective, customized treatment via precision medicine. Thanks to the way it integrates genomics with lab results and EHRs (including pathology and imaging), providers can "see" individual patient's unique physical status with much greater clarity. Precision medicine improves a supervising doctor's ability to forecast disease in their patients and provide more customized treatment and medication. Such customization is based on genomic data that predicts biological patterns, which will impact the efficacy of a treatment and/or medication for an individual patient. This ability to forecast patients' responses to treatment will allow providers to treat them more effectively. Doing so means healthcare costs can be significantly reduced by eliminating unnecessary lab tests or ineffective medicine and treatments.

Payers Need to Network

Large payers need to proactively network to create lines of communication with different players being impacted by precision medicine. In the case of new drug development, for example, payers must network with drug manufacturers, the FDA, and pharmacy benefit managers. Such communication will help ensure the pharma market is driven by the clinical effectiveness of existing drugs plus convey a more effective demand for new drugs.

Overall, this networking strategy makes good business sense since it will serve to connect the separate segments of the current value chain. Improving lines of communication will also help payers work with the FDA and drug manufacturers to structure quality-control systems for genetic testing. Enterprise-level payers who are positioning themselves to capture and sustain the value of precision medicine in these ways will need to focus on areas that will establish and drive *efficiency*. The following chart depicts an example of an effective healthcare value chain:

The medical race to unlock the value of precision medicine with genomics is gaining momentum. Fueled by consumer interest in genetic testing, increasing use of genomics' more personalized treatment is an important aspect of the digital health-tech revolution. Like each person's genome, the course of their disease—including its onset, its course, and how it might respond to drugs or other interventions—is different too. Genomics' ability to see and utilize the complete DNA sequence unique to each person is driving precision medicine's valuable new testing and treatment options.

MY EXECUTIVE TAKEAWAY

Tech pioneers need to know how precision medicine is impacting payers to meet their strategic interests. Integrating precision medicine into patient care is getting easier as structured clinical and technical support is being put in place. As a result, those watching healthcare's digital transformation predict genomic testing results will soon become just as common as drug-drug and drug-allergy results in

EHRs.[78] Even the current multimillion-dollar price tag of developing and refining expensive gene and cell therapies/drugs will ultimately prove it's worth the investment cost. Returns from restored patient health and from huge cost savings across the healthcare industry will accrue as many chronic diseases are cured. To access those savings, healthcare players need to take the following steps:

Eliminate Payment Silos. Health industry leaders need to eliminate payment silos and individual incentives, which risk prioritizing commercialization over patient health. Doing that successfully will require close partnerships within the healthcare ecosystem in order to scale, build, and integrate precision medicine–based solutions within existing clinical care models.

Deliver Intelligent Data Management. Since payer insurance data is higher in volume and quality compared to other stakeholders, payers need to lead the development of standards for the intake and management of the genetic data used in precision medicine. That will mean setting up secure storage mechanisms via cloud infrastructures or comparable alternatives. These are needed to securely house electronic medical records, longitudinal clinical data, and the genetic data precision medicine requires to provide actionable insights. The value of those insights is lost, however, if providers don't have the training or motivation to integrate them into their decision-making process.

Make Coverage Accessible. Providers wanting to use precision medicine to help their patients are looking to payers to standardize their coverage determinations. They also need payers to lead the way to modernize billing, medical coding, and documentation issues so that they know what options they can afford to offer their

---

78   R H Dolin et al., "A Pharmacogenomics Clinical Decision Support Service Based on FHIR and CDS Hooks," PubMed.gov, accessed January 2023, https://www.ncbi.nlm. nih.gov/pubmed/30605914.

patients. Since payers are such major stakeholders in the healthcare industry, providers and patients look to them to unlock precision medicine's potential.

Precision medicine only became possible after AI made it possible to analyze vast amounts of biological and digital data. Thanks to AI's ability to interpret and act upon big data patterns, AI technology is being incorporated into every aspect of digital health technology. In the chapter ahead, I'll show savvy entrepreneurs how it's being deployed throughout the health sector.

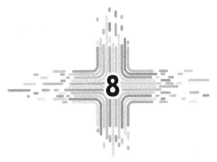

ARTIFICIAL INTELLIGENCE, NOT ARTIFICIAL CARE

How AI Benefits Healthcare

Fear of transparency and capitalism of healthcare are some of the biggest obstacles to innovation. As more data becomes available and as more data gets digitized, this will change.

—ANTHONY FERNANDO, CEO, ASENSUS SURGICAL

No, robots aren't going to take over your job in healthcare, but they just might help all of us in the health industry avoid burnout. The use of AI is sparking an explosion of innovation—not by replacing people but by optimizing their efforts in ways that save time, money, and *lives*. One example of this machine-human partnering is the way the AI speech recognition software Corti is used by Emergency Medical Technicians (EMTs) to do just that. It's being used by Boston Emergency Medical Services (Boston EMS) to cut an hour-long emergency response down to fifteen minutes so that they can help more people.

When Boston EMS receives call for an ambulance, the AI assistant Corti will be on the line. It uses speech recognition software to transcribe the conversation so that dispatchers don't have to type it in. And Corti will also be using machine learning to analyze words and a host of background sounds as clues that (may or may not) point to a cardiac arrest diagnosis. While in transit, the EMT gets alerts from Corti in real time so that they know what to do the minute they arrive. In the EMS world, minutes and seconds can determine whether a patient survives or not. Cardiac arrest is a case in point. When someone's heart stops, their chance of survival falls by 10 percent each minute they don't receive rapid medical intervention. Just being able to recognize cardiac arrest by phone is challenging for emergency dispatchers when they're forced to make sense of symptoms being described by a panicking friend or relative.

This lifesaving application is just one of the hundreds of ways AI is already benefiting all of healthcare's 5P stakeholders. AI can speed consumer access to customized medical information, improve clinical workflows and operations, and also assist medical and nonmedical staff with repetitive tasks. In fact, the growth of AI technology is accelerating the digital tech transformation of healthcare as it reshapes the industry in many medical fields and specialties. The different aspects of AI, including machine learning (ML), natural language processing (NLP), and deep learning (DL), enable healthcare stakeholders and medical professionals to identify health needs and solutions faster and more accurately. These benefits are the result of AI's ability to rapidly interpret big data patterns and make informed medical or business decisions more quickly.

LET THE AI DO IT

As president and CEO of Asensus Surgical, Anthony Fernando is keenly aware of the way AI is accelerating the digital health transformation of medicine. His company is at the forefront of AI-driven robotics for surgery and is pioneering a new era of performance-guided surgery. By digitizing the interface between the surgeon and the patient, the company's assistive AI has been able to provide improved outcomes with better surgical control during procedures.

When I asked the Asensus Surgical CEO what he considered to be the biggest obstacle for health-tech innovation, Anthony didn't hesitate before replying.

"Fear of transparency and capitalism of healthcare are some of the biggest obstacles to innovation. As more data becomes available and as more data gets digitized, this will change."

Like I had, I knew the CEO must have faced regulatory hurdles while building his innovative healthcare company. But when I asked him (digitally) how he dealt with those, I could almost see him shrug.

> In my mind, the regulatory piece is not that hard to solve if you know what you're doing. First, read the Code of Federal Regulations document. It tells you everything you need to know. But in case you're still not sure, ask yourself, *What does a regulator want?* They want to make sure your product is safe and effective. So it's your job to do the work to prove it in a robust manner. As investors, KOLs, and others get involved, the line of sight gets very cloudy fast, and you need to stay the course with the original goal and purpose to realize it.

I mentally nodded in agreement, having pursued the same strategy when creating my own companies. Likewise, I agreed with Anthony's high-level view of how US health systems differed from those outside of the country.

AI IS TRANSFORMING HEALTHCARE

These insights create perspective on how much the health industry has changed during the ongoing digital health transformation in the realm of AI-driven medical robotics. Developing AI for use in robotic-assisted surgery took longer than in other medical applications. But thanks to rapid developments in the needed computational technology, AI is already being used to supplement the skill of human surgeons. And although the potential of the surgeon-patient-computer link is a long way from being fully realized, the use of AI in surgery is already driving significant changes for surgical procedures.

Such innovation is only possible because AI "speaks" the digital language used by the new software and robotic devices used in those procedures. When combined with AI-driven robotic assistance, the use of computed tomography (CT), ultrasound and magnetic resonance imaging (MRI), and minimally invasive surgery (MIS) has resulted in decreased surgical trauma and improved patient recovery. In MIS, computer-assisted intraoperative guidance has always been regarded as the essential foundation. Now, AI's learning strategies are being implemented in several areas of MIS, such as more accurate tissue tracking, to prevent the problem of deformation during MIS intraoperative guidance and navigation. Since tissue deformation can't be accurately depicted with improvised representations, scientists have developed an online, AI algorithm-based learning framework that can identify the appropriate tracking method for in vivo practice.

AI's algorithms enable machines to perform cognitive functions (e.g., problem-solving and decision-making) and to engage in ML and NLP in a way that's forever changed healthcare.

ML and DL are both types of AI. In short, ML is AI that can automatically adapt with minimal human interference. DL is a subset that mimics the learning process of the human brain. An example of that mimicry is the way an AI algorithm is designed to identify and label certain data patterns, but it's NLP that allows an algorithm to isolate relevant data. With DL, as other forms of AI, the data is analyzed and interpreted with the help of computers. The impact of these tools is huge. A Frost & Sullivan analysis indicated AI and cognitive computing systems in healthcare were estimated to account for $6.7 billion in 2021 compared to $811 million in 2015.[79]

AI BENEFITS ALL HEALTHCARE STAKEHOLDERS

That accelerating trend isn't surprising considering how the use of AI is directly or indirectly supporting all healthcare stakeholders. By using AI, for example, teams of clinicians, researchers, or data managers involved in clinical trials can speed up the process of medical coding search and confirmation—a process crucial to conducting and concluding clinical studies. Clinicians can also improve and customize patient care by using AI to comb through medical data to predict or diagnose disease faster and more accurately. And healthcare payers can personalize their health plans by connecting a virtual agent via conversational AI with members interested in customized health solutions. The following chart depicts the many ways AI is already being used to make health systems more efficient with generative AI. This generative AI creates various types of content, such as text, imagery, audio, and synthetic data.

---

79   "From $600M to $6 Billion, Artificial Intelligence Systems Poised for 'Dramatic' Market Expansion in Healthcare," Frost & Sullivan, March 12, 2019, https://www.frost. com/news/press-releases/600-m-6-billion-artificial-intelligence-systems-poised-dramatic-market-expansion-healthcare/.

GENERATIVE AI

HIGH FLUENCY

| | Translating medical records written by physicians/ nurses to layman terms | | Behavioral health chat bots to address therapist shortages / Transitions of care for discharge summary |

- Translating medical records written by physicians/ nurses to layman terms

- Behavioral health chat bots to address therapist shortages
- Transitions of care for discharge summary

| LOW ACCURACY | | | HIGH ACCURACY |

- Creating a longitudinal medical record into a short summary

- Writing a recommendation
- Creating a healthcare marketing campaign
- Engagement campaigns in second grade reading level

- Creating business presentations
- Ingest payment policy
- Prior authorization workforce

- Doctor recommendations
- Medical treatment recommendations
- DTC healthcare purchases

LOW ACCURACY   **HIGH ACCURACY**

- Underwriting and pricing for

  What's my co-pay excluded?

  Did I reach my deductible?

- Finding doctors who are in network
- Scheduling appointments

- Supporting data for busienss decisions
- Translating symptoms to likely diagnosis

LOW FLUENCY

The Fluency and Accuracy of AI: The concepts of high fluency versus high accuracy are the two ways to assess generative AI.

As AI continues to transform healthcare, it's also being used to support health equity. Healthcare research now has the potential to use AI and ML to eliminate biased outcomes based on race, ethnicity, or gender. Training AI and ML algorithms to remove such biases is completely doable and necessary to produce data accuracy. Although many clinical trial guidelines and diagnostic tests factor in a patient's race and ethnicity, it's not known whether the inclusion of this data actually reduces or increases universal health inequities. Fortunately, ML comprises a set of methods enabling computers to learn from the data they process. This means that, at least in principle, trainable ML algorithms can provide unbiased health predictions—based solely on impartial analysis of healthcare data. Since that's the case, the AI and ML industry is responsible to design healthcare systems and tools that ensure fairness and equality in data science and clinical studies in order to deliver the best possible health outcomes. You get the idea. AI's extensive use in healthcare will continue to expand.

THE POWER OF AI FOR SURGERY

Even before AI-assisted surgery, AI was being used to enhance preoperative planning by providing better analysis of images in patient medical records. DL algorithms, for example, were able to identify abnormalities such as calvarial fracture, intracranial hemorrhage, and midline shift from CT scans. This ML has made emergency care for these complex abnormalities possible and foreshadows the future use of AI in the automation of triage itself. The AI in DL Recurrent Neural Networks (RNN) is also generating improved results (compared to standard clinical reference tools) when used to predict renal failure or mortality and postoperative bleeding after cardio surgery. These predictions are based on clinical data that's automatically collected and analyzed without manual processing, so it can preemptively help more vulnerable patients receive the kind of critical care they need.

AI Controls Robotic Surgical Assistants

AI-driven surgical robots are helping surgeons improve their skills and perform better during procedures. Asensus Surgical, for example, has a performance-guided laparoscopic AI robot that can digitally convey essential information, such as tissue size, back to surgeons, negating the need for a physical measuring tape. As designed, these are successfully assisting surgeons with the manipulation and positioning of their surgical instruments during operations.

A variety of computer-driven robotic devices now allow surgeons to focus on the more complex aspects of a surgery by freeing them from repetitive tasks. The efficiency achieved by robotic assistance not only lowers healthcare expenditures but also produces better patient outcomes by decreasing fluctuations in surgeons' dexterity during procedures.

Surgical robots can also use ML programs to browse through millions of datasets to help identify critical insights and state-of-the-art practices for a particular condition and suggest the best ones. But these robotic assistants won't replace humans because surgeons are needed to program these robots by demonstrating the correct hand movements during every kind of surgical procedure. During this kind of Learning from Demonstration (LfD), it's necessary to "train" robots in stages before they can independently conduct new tasks. In the first stage, LfD splits a complex surgical task into several subtasks and basic gestures. In a second stage, surgical robots recognize, model, and conduct the subtasks in a sequential mode appropriate to a specific procedure.

Teaching autonomous robots the surgical tasks they need to master is a difficult endeavor, especially in minimally invasive surgery. To accelerate the process, the JHU-ISI Gesture and Skill Assessment Working Set (JIGSAWS) has been developed as the first public benchmark for a dataset capturing surgical activity. It features kinematic data and synchronized video for three standard surgery tasks conducted by Johns Hopkins University surgeons with different surgical skill levels. The kinematics and stereo video recorded and analyzed surgeons performing the subtasks of suturing, needle passing, and knot tying—the smallest movements used during the significant segments of different surgeries.

For many surgical tasks, Reinforcement Learning (RL) is an ML paradigm that's used to solve subtasks, such as tube insertion and soft tissue manipulation. These actions are difficult to render into precise analytical models. So RL algorithms help solve that problem by using partially formatted demonstrations. This reduces the time needed for the learning process because ML isn't starting from zero.

Touchless Surgical Control of Robots

Humans and AI-directed robots can now interact to operate surgical robots through touchless manipulation. Such manipulation is possible by head or hand movements, through speech and voice recognition, or even a surgeon's gaze. FAceMOUSe is one example of this kind of innovation. Directed by surgeons' head movements alone, this device remotely controls a robotic laparoscope using the face gestures of the surgeon to simply and accurately control the motion of the laparoscope. This kind of noninvasive and nonverbal cooperation between humans and robots for various surgical procedures will soon be a standard operating procedure. The following examples provide a glimpse into how that's currently happening.

Blood vessel suturing can now be performed using an AI-driven robot for microsurgery intervention. In 2017, Maastricht University

Medical Center in the Netherlands used a surgical robot to suture blood vessels between 0.03 and 0.08 millimeters in a patient affected by lymphedema. This chronic condition is often a side effect that occurs during treatment of breast cancer and causes swelling as a result of fluids building up. Directed by a surgeon, the robotic "hands" created by Microsure successfully compensated for the slight but inevitable tremble in a human surgeon's hands and completed the surgery using smaller and more accurate movements.

Hair restoration is presently being done with surgical robots that harvest hair follicles and graft them into precise areas of the scalp with the help of AI algorithms. Because these robots conduct MIS without requiring surgical removal of a donor area, it eliminates the need for a hair transplant surgeon to manually extract one follicle at a time. The procedure time is greatly reduced as a result.

Cardiac surgery is being conducted with the Da Vinci medical robot through very small chest incisions that are cut with robot-manipulated tools and very small instruments. This cardio robotic surgery is being successfully used for different heart-related procedures, such as coronary artery bypass, valve surgery, cardiac tissue ablation, tumor removal, and heart defect repair.

Surgical nursing functions can now be completed with Gestonurse, a robotic assistant that's been designed to hand surgical instruments to surgeons in the operating room. Designed to reduce the negative impact of human error during surgery, the robot uses fingertip recognition and gesture deduction for manipulating the needed instruments.

These examples show AI-driven robotic surgery is expanding rapidly as surgeons and scientists join forces to capture, process, and classify data across each phase of clinical care. Development has proceeded to the point that surgical robots and surgeon-robot collaborations are spurring questions about the legal status of independent robots and when they cease to be a simple AI-driven device as opposed to being dependent on a surgeon for their operational efficacy. Even before a surgical procedure, clinicians welcome the way AI can be used as a tool to assist with triage, providing enhanced medical analysis of images and scans. This makes it easier for radiologists and cardiologists to prioritize critical cases and avoid errors reading EHRs to establish more precise diagnoses.

AI Speeds Genetic Medicine Discovery and Development

Discovering and developing genetic medicines have accelerated rapidly with the help of AI's ability to detect and analyze altered molecular phenotypes, such as protein binding, that predict the likelihood of genetic disease. After collecting data on all identified compounds and biomarkers during clinical trials, this data can be processed by an AI system to discover new methods to fix the consequences of genetic mutations. Deep Genomics is one company designing this kind of proprietary AI system, and they're using it to help lower the cost of developing customized therapies for people suffering from rare, complex, and inherited diseases.

With the help of AI, company tests identify compounds enabling them to develop faster genetic medicine for conditions with high unmet need. The company's Project Saturn drug system, for example, monitors cell biology to unlock greater potential treatments and therapies. It uses AI molecular biology that can assess more than 69 billion oligonucleotide molecules in silico (computer modeling or computer simulation) against one million target sites to identify and develop new genetic medicines.

AI Lowers Drug Development Costs

In yet another profitable application of AI in healthcare, AI-enhanced supercomputers are helping with drug development. AI can analyze databases of molecular structures to assess which ones could yield a potentially effective medicine for a particular disease. Using AI technology similar to the one that makes cars drive by themselves, the company Atomwise has developed a computer platform to predict the bioactivity of molecules for the purpose of drug discovery. Called AtomNet, the AI-driven platform is able to predict the binding of small molecules to proteins by analyzing hints from millions of experimental measurements and thousands of protein structures. This process reduces the cost of developing medicine by enabling convolutional neural networks to identify safe and effective drug candidates from database searches.

A similar AI application aided the development of a treatment for the Ebola virus in 2015 during the West African Ebola virus outbreak that year. Atomwise partnered with IBM and the University of Toronto to screen the top compounds capable of binding to a glycoprotein that would prevent Ebola virus penetration into cells in an in vivo test (one conducted in the living body of an animal or plant). As incredible as it sounds, this AI analysis, search, and selection of an effective compound occurred *in less than a day*—a process that would normally take months or years.[80]

As AI algorithms identify new drugs, they can trace drugs' toxic potential and mechanisms of action as well. By applying AI technology this way, the pharmaceutical company Recursion Pharmaceuticals created a drug discovery platform to repurpose existing drugs and

---

80 "New Ebola Treatment Using Artificial Intelligence," Atomwise, March 24, 2015, https://www.atomwise.com/2015/03/24/new-ebola-treatment-using-artificial-intelligence/.

bioactive compounds.[81] Identifying new uses for known drugs is an appealing strategy for big pharma companies since it's less expensive to repurpose and reposition existing drugs instead of creating them from scratch. By combining AI tools and automation advances with the best elements of biology, data science, and chemistry, the founding company has been able to generate and process around 80 terabytes of biological data across 1.5 million experiments weekly—an impossible feat without AI's ML attribute.

AI Data Analysis Aids Providers

Clinicians providing quality, patient-centered care often struggle to stay up-to-date on the latest medical advances. Too much research time is spent sorting through piles of paper-formatted EHRs, trying to access their patients' medical records. Now time-strapped clinicians are getting help with from AI's ML technology. After quickly scanning EHRs and biomedical data that's been curated by medical units and medical professionals, AI is able to provide clinicians with prompt, reliable answers.

It's an AI innovation that's critically needed. Since many patients' medical records are still stored as complicated, unstructured data, it's difficult to interpret and access. Now AI can seek, collect, store, and standardize that medical data, so clinicians can tailor accurate treatment plans and medicine for their patients more quickly and easily. Not only that, AI's ability to analyze data is being used to predict the likelihood of patients' medical outcomes.

---

81 "Recursion Pharmaceuticals Raises $13M to Discover Drugs Using Artificial Intelligence," Business Wire, October 3, 2016, https://www.businesswire.com/news/home/20161003005212/en/Recursion-Pharmaceuticals-Raises-13M-Discover-Drugs-Artificial.

AI-Driven Data for Predictive Analytics

Using AI to turn EHRs into a predictive tool fosters more successful patient outcomes by helping steer clinicians' workflows, medical decisions, and treatment plans in the right direction. AI is no medical "crystal ball," but NLP and ML *can* read a patient's entire medical history in real time. By cross-referencing their medical/family history with symptoms and chronic infections, AI can be used as a predictive analytics tool. It can help catch and treat a patient's disease before it becomes life threatening.

In essence, AI is showing chronic disease progression can be forecast ahead of time and tracked in real time. CloudMedX is a company enabling such forecasting. It leverages AI's ability to decode unstructured data stored in the form of EHRs, clinician notes, discharge summaries, diagnoses, and hospital records. The company's AI-enabled approach is giving clinicians the early, accurate diagnostic edge they need to more effectively combat high-risk diseases, such as renal failure, pneumonia, congestive heart failure, hypertension, liver cancer, diabetes, orthopedic surgery, and stroke.

AI Aids Kidney Disease Diagnosis

Another important AI advancement is the way it's helping providers perform the difficult task of detecting Acute Kidney Injury (AKI) before patients deteriorate. In the case of AKI, that can happen so fast; the condition has the potential of becoming life threatening before it's diagnosed. With an estimated 11 percent of deaths in hospitals following a failure to identify and treat patients with AKI, the early prediction and treatment of these cases can have a huge impact on saving those lives or preventing lifelong treatment and the cost of kidney dialysis.[82]

---

82 "Safer Care for the Acutely Ill Patient: Learning from Serious Incidents," DocPlayer. net, accessed January 2023, https://docplayer.net/19744378-Safer-care-for-the-acutely-ill-patient-learning-from-serious-incidents.html.

In 2019, the Department of Veterans Affairs (VA) and DeepMind Health created an AI tool using ML that can predict more than 90 percent of acute AKI cases forty-eight hours earlier than traditional care methods.[83] The partnership between VA and DeepMind Health continues with the goal of helping clinicians by installing this ML tool in medical units along with a user-friendly platform to assist their AKI treatment decisions for veterans suffering from the disease.

AI for Cancer Research and Treatment

To help clinicians make decisions about radiation therapy for cancer patients, Oncora Medical has developed a platform that collects patients' relevant medical data in a searchable digital database. Clinicians can access it to see detailed information about patients' oncology outcomes, data, and imaging to evaluate the quality of their past care and optimize their future treatments. Being able to research the platform's integrated EHRs and automatically generated clinical notes reduces the time clinicians spend managing patient documentation. The result is improved medical operations and better health outcomes during and after cancer treatment.

A CEO CASE IN POINT

As founder and CEO of the venture capital firm Breyer Capital, Jim Breyer is someone with deep insight into the investment potential of AI in healthcare. He's confident that AI will help companies, institutions, and individuals accomplish extraordinary things for the betterment of humanity. As an early investor in AI-driven technology, he's been investing in entrepreneurs and teams working at the intersection

---

83   "VA, DeepMind Develop Machine Learning System to Predict Life-Threatening Disease before It Appears," U.S. Department of Veterans Affairs, May 21, 2019, https://www.va.gov/opa/pressrel/pressrelease.cfm?id=5287.

of AI, healthcare, and life sciences. So it makes sense to listen to his projections about the future of the technology.

He admits AI algorithms are still in their early stages. But he predicts, "We can expect to see many more research breakthroughs in the coming months and years. Especially as data sets become larger and more accessible, and computational power becomes more affordable, AI applications will become more powerful and ubiquitous."[84] The firm has continued to explore how AI can transform diagnostic workflows, drug discovery or development, and clinical trials. At the same time, they've planted new ventures in leading-edge areas, such as quantum technologies and decentralized science, at their earliest stages.

MY EXECUTIVE TAKEAWAY

Investing in AI-related innovations will create hundreds of billions of dollars of market cap by venture-backed startups. More importantly, if ethically and effectively harnessed, these AI breakthroughs will improve patients' overall experiences and outcomes. Although many people think AI will make medicine less humane, since devices and algorithms don't feel compassion in the same way that humans do, they needn't worry. Better technology will allow doctors to spend *more time caring for patients* and providing the personalized care patients value most.

> ➤ Health leaders would be well advised to invest in companies leveraging computation for harvesting insights from proteomics, metabolomics, genomics, and clinical and claims data.

---

84   Jim Breyer, "Breyer Capital's Healthcare AI Investment Thesis: Learnings and Predictions," Medium, December 2, 2021, https://medium.com/@jimbreyer/breyer-capitals-healthcare-ai-investment-thesis-learnings-and-predictions-december-2021-update-45e2e81b0c86.

➢ Key factors indicating a good investment opportunity include the almost universal adoption of EHR, regulatory progress in data interoperability, and rapidly declining costs of genetic sequencing.

➢ Likewise, it's important that health leaders stay abreast of generative AI approaches as they continue to evolve. Examples include GPT-3, DALL-E, and AlphaFold.

Thanks to the way AI can analyze huge amounts of data and images at high speed, I'm optimistic about how it will continue to drive future innovation. Its algorithms are able to compare, detect, and glean crucial insights from complex, nearly invisible patterns and interconnections. Those AI abilities are essential to an evolving Internet of Medical Things (IoMT) and the RPM that depends on it. In the chapter ahead, I'll discuss how those interdependent digital health technologies are already transforming healthcare in a way that significantly benefits patients, providers, and payers.

WI-FI WELLNESS

Keeping Tabs with
Remote Patient Monitoring

*We have an opportunity to create a patient-physician-data care
loop enabled by intelligent monitoring of vital signs ...*

—BRIDGET ROSS, CHRONISENSE MEDICAL CEO

Smart healthcare investors rely on the business adage "follow the money." That being the case, it's important to note $9.4 billion were wagered on US digital health startups in 2020. It was the highest amount ever invested in digital health companies. In the third quarter alone, savvy industry insiders spent $4 billion to indicate they knew digital health tech was a safe bet.[85] And even though the billions already invested weren't all spent on RPM tech *per se*, it shows overall demand for new Digital Therapeutics Technology (DTx) is high in the form of digital tools, solutions, and products, which include those devices.

Bridget Ross, CEO of *ChroniSense Medical*, who is coming off a recently secured Series A fundraising round, put it this way in a conversation with me:

---

85   Elaine Wang and Sean Day, "Q3 2020 Digital Health Funding Already Sets a New Annual Record," Rock Health, October 14, 2020, https://rockhealth.com/insights/q3-2020-digital-health-funding-already-sets-a-new-annual-record/.

> Our goal is to bring chronic care patient management into the twenty-first century by commercializing medical-grade solutions. We have an opportunity to create a patient-physician-data care loop enabled by intelligent monitoring of vital signs including blood pressure (BP), a health parameter so far elusive to most technology offerings.
>
> We see Polso CONNECT, our RPM technology, as a key enabler of the shift toward virtual chronic care and the shift toward decentralized clinical trials, both high growth areas in need of medical-grade remote patient monitoring solutions.

Monitoring blood pressure is an important step in virtual chronic care because uncontrolled high blood pressure can cause stroke, heart failure, and kidney failure. The management of uncontrolled hypertension is thought to be the Holy Grail in RPM, and it's next on the list of clearances that ChroniSense Medical's CEO and her team are pursuing. "We have IP to support our unique approach to BP measurement," she told me, "because our sensor uses radial artery (underside of the wrist) signal acquisition to ensure robust measurement and we have clinical trial data to back this up."

DIRECT-TO-CONSUMER RPM IS HERE TO STAY

On the consumer side of RPM, WHOOP founder and CEO Will Ahmed's fitness tracker is an example of what's unfolding in the direct-to-consumer (DTC) market. He raised more than $400 million from top investors to develop a fitness tracker that optimizes human performance and health by measuring exercise strain, recovery, and sleep. His next-generation wearable technology has garnered wide appeal, and it's being used by a diverse group of consumers, ranging from professional athletes to fitness enthusiasts, executives, military personnel, and healthcare workers. Prior to its release, the WHOOP CEO laid out the principles undergirding the development of the device in his book, *The Feedback Tool: Measuring Fitness, Intensity, and Recovery.*

Like many other industry stakeholders, he sees the fact that the US spends more money (per person) on healthcare than any other country in the world as one of the biggest issues facing our healthcare system.

"This is largely due to the US healthcare system's focus on curative medicine and the need to treat a patient *after* an injury or illness has already occurred," Ahmed explained. He described the impact of that approach and how it can be corrected:

> This is tremendously costly. At WHOOP, we believe health monitoring can shift the balance in healthcare to preventative efforts. We are empowering people to take control of their own health through our industry-leading wearable technology and 24/7 coaching. We see tremendous results: after using WHOOP for ten weeks, members get more sleep, have lower resting heart rates, exercise more frequently, and have higher heart rate variability. All of these improvements lead to better health. Focusing on preventative health will help our healthcare system save an enormous amount of money and, most importantly, create better outcomes for people.

Since better health outcomes are the primary objective of the digital healthcare transformation, WHOOP's success should inspire other innovative entrepreneurs.

Ahmed's advice?

> Be ambitious and keep going. At WHOOP, one of our internal guidelines is to "move at an uncomfortable pace." The health-care industry has many large, legacy players with huge budgets. The best entrepreneurs and startups will succeed when they can move quicker than their opponents and demonstrate to payers and customers the effectiveness of their products.

WHOOP's fitness tracker is just one of a host of consumer and medical RPM devices that function as wearable remote-monitoring tools that can measure a wearer's vital signs, allowing them (plus a coach or clinician) to "hear" from their own bodies and respond appropriately. Whether it's used as a medical tool or a consumer tool, RPM is helping ameliorate the chronic disease epidemic that's worsening Americans' health and the condition of healthcare itself. RPM bucks this trend by facilitating better care of patients who already have some level of chronic disease and helps block disease in those that don't. And it's this preventive effect that's key to RPM benefiting *all* of healthcare's 5P stakeholders through better outcomes and lower costs.

REMOTE MONITORING BENEFITS STAKEHOLDERS

Investors have been able to verify that RPM devices really work as intended in studies proving the efficacy of remote health monitoring devices (either used as stand-alone solutions or combined with traditional medical protocols). These findings show positive results in various diseases or disorders such as asthma,[86]

---

86 Meredith Barrett, Veronica Combs, Jason G. Su, Kelly Henderson, Michael Tuffli; AIR Louisville Collaborative, "AIR Louisville: Addressing Asthma with Technology, Crowdsourcing, Cross-Sector Collaboration, and Policy," *Health Affairs* 37, no. 4 (2018): 525–534, https://pubmed.ncbi.nlm.nih.gov/29608361/.

cancer,[87] and insomnia.[88] Like other types of transformative healthcare DTx, remote-monitoring devices rely on gathering and analyzing digital data that's sent and received via the internet and smartphones. Such analysis provides the insights needed for customizing many types of wearable DTx hardware that lower costs and increase profitability. So it's not surprising they've been embraced by healthcare stakeholders, considering the benefits:

- *Physicians/providers* benefit from healthcare DTx that enables them to monitor and manage patient health and patient networks more conveniently, efficiently, and effectively. When physicians use medical-grade (FDA-cleared) devices for monitoring and decision-making, their time and expertise can be compensated by private and public payers' Current Procedural Terminology (CPT) payment codes.

- *Patients/consumers* benefit from interactive or wearable healthcare DTx devices that promote disease prevention by monitoring their vital signs and motivating them to take more responsibility and control over their health status.

- *Private employer payers* benefit from the way wearable DTx boosts health to reduce the financial impact of lost productivity when employees or their family members are sick.

---

87   Fabrice Denis, Ethan Basch, Anne-Lise Septans, Jaafar Bennouna, Thierry Urban, Amylou C. Dueck, and Christophe Letellier, "Two-Year Survival Comparing Web-Based Symptom Monitoring vs Routine Surveillance Following Treatment for Lung Cancer," *JAMA* 321 (2019): 306–307, https://pubmed.ncbi.nlm.nih.gov/30667494/.

88   Daniel Freeman, et al., "The Effects of Improving Sleep on Mental Health (OASIS): A Randomised Controlled Trial with Mediation Analysis," *Lancet Psychiatry* 4 (2017): 749–758, https://pubmed.ncbi.nlm.nih.gov/28888927/.

- *Public payers* benefit from lower costs as healthier beneficiaries have less chronic illness because of the way DTx, in the form of RPM, promotes better health and quality of life for beneficiaries. The following chart shows how companies are leveraging RPM.

PERSPECTIVE ON DIGITAL HEALTH OPPORTUNITY BY STAKEHOLDER GROUP

STAKEHOLDER		DIGITAL HEALTH & RPM OPPORTUNITY
Providers	Capitated/ at-risk	Focused on demonstrable ROI at scale to justify investment. Opportunity to deploy RPM in value-based pricing models once efficacy demonstrated
	Fee For Service	Adoption largely driven by reimbursement. Telemedicine usage highly sensitive to payer reimbursement; remote monitoring adoption will largely be driven by CMS RPM reimbursement, with providers focused on solutions that improve patient outcomes
Pharma Value Chain	Pharmacos	Reinventing customer engagement strategies (patient and provider) given digital disruption/opportunities—both organically and through partnerships; evolution of data analytic approaches given proliferation of customer data (e.g., omnichannel)
Payers		Payers looking for digital health upsell capabilities for ASO customers for ASO customers; limited willingness to adopt at scale for fully-insured plans until cost savings/outcomes improvements are demonstrated at scale
Employers	Benefits Innovators	High adoption rate of digital health solutions; often willing to work with multiple solution/service providers directly and integrate offerings
	Other Segments	Moderate adoption rate; typically looking for ~breakeven ROI, and more likely to purchase payer-offered digital health solution bundle vs. working directly with multiple solution/ service providers
Digital Health Solution/Service Providers		Rapidly growing market, driven by significant investment and adoption. Recognition that partnerships are critical to achieve required solution/service breadth

Source: Mathis Friesdorf et al., "Digital Health Ecosystems: A Payer Perspective," mckinsey.com, August 2, 2019, https://www.mckinsey.com/industries/healthcare/our-insights/digital-health-ecosystems-a-payer-perspective.
"McKinsey on Healthcare: Weathering the Storm," mckinsey.com, 2022, https://www.mckinsey.com/industries/healthcare/our-insights/mckinsey-on-healthcare-weathering-the-storm.

How Companies Are Leveraging RPM

WEARABLE TECHNOLOGY IN GROWTH MODE

As a physician, it's been exciting to watch and participate in the exponential development and deployment of wearable health technology products. Most of these innovations represent true breakthroughs in the prevention and treatment of illness, providing care in ways never before possible. The following examples provide a glimpse of the breadth of health issues being addressed by RPM:

- In Louisville, Kentucky, it's been documented that wearable devices made by AIR Louisville can be successfully used to monitor local air quality, measure pollutants, and identify hotspots for residents with respiratory problems.[89]

- Cyrcadia Health has developed Cyrcadia Breast Monitor, an intelligent patch that can detect early signs of breast cancer and transmit the information to a lab for analysis.[90]

- Wearable medical alert monitors like Vios are extending greater mobility and independence to the elderly and impaired.[91]

- Polso VSM, a wrist-worn, multi-vital sign-measuring device, will create better care and outcomes for patients living with chronic conditions, such as hypertension, heart failure, COPD, and kidney disease.

---

89 Meredith Barrett, Veronica Combs, Jason G. Su, Kelly Henderson, and Michael Tuffli, "AIR Louisville: Addressing Asthma with Technology, Crowdsourcing, Cross-Sector Collaboration, and Policy," *Health Affairs* 37 (2018), https://www.healthaffairs.org/doi/abs/10.1377/hlthaff.2017.1315.

90 Vinitha Sree S., et al., "An Introduction to the Cyrcadia Breast Monitor: A Wearable Breast Health Monitoring Device," *Computer Methods and Programs in Biomedicine* 197: 105758, https://pubmed.ncbi.nlm.nih.gov/33007593/.

91 "Leverage Technology to Improve Patient Care and Reduce Operational Costs," Vios Medical, https://www.viosmedical.com/product/?gclid=Cj0KCQiAsdKbBhDHARIsANJ6-jciiAZMCWtmrNZNcBcBxEApaiVj6niV-FQCMMcQeipfjGLNgbh2qS0aAvaFEALw_wcB.

- Smart tattoos that contain flexible electronic sensors are being developed to monitor heart and brain activity, sleep disorders, and muscle function. While these are temporary, more permanent inks are being explored.

- A smartwatch for people with Parkinson's disease tracks symptoms and transmits the data so that more personalized treatment plans can be developed.[92]

IOMT MAKES DIGITAL HEALTHCARE THERAPEUTICS POSSIBLE

The digital connectivity of IoMT is what's making wearable health technology and RPM possible. Thanks to the way this ecosystem of connected medical devices collects and transmits data from users and their environments, providers can increasingly monitor and treat their patients remotely. This infrastructure of intelligent medical devices enables clinicians to diagnose and treat their patients more effectively with each new innovation. Ranging from inhalers and thermometers to chatbots and wearable biosensors, these smart medical devices are dramatically impacting patients' health outcomes. Fortunately, reimbursement for using RPM is available as a subsector of telehealth as indicated in the following two RPM CPT code charts:

---

92   "NHS Smartwatch for Parkinson's Patients Hailed as 'Lifechang-ing,'" Guardian, https://www.theguardian.com/society/2022/apr/16/nhs-smartwatch-for-parkinsons-patients-hailed-as-lifechanging.

RPM CPT CODES

KEY DEFINITIONS

Remote Patient Monitoring	Use of digital technologies to monitor and capture medical data
Current Procedural Terminology Codes	Offers doctors and healthcare providers a uniform language for coding medical services and procedures

BACKGROUND INFORMATION

RPM is a subsector of telehealth (the use of electronics to provide long-distance clinical)

The CPT coding system ensures healthcare providers are correctly logging and billing procedures for the right patient

Three categories of CPT codes:

Category I: Medical Billing and Revenue Cycle Management

Category II: Reporting Performance measures reducing the necessity for chart review and medical records abstraction

Category III: Emerging and experimental technologies, services and procedures

IMPACT OF RPM CPT CODES ON HEALTHTECH

Healthtech startups can design their products to match previous CPT codes to make it easier for hospitals to bill, record and expand upon

Ex: Spark Neuro designed their product to match a high-value CPT code offering a $400 reimbursement to doctors

Source: https://streamlinehealth.net/cpt-codes/, https://blog.prevounce.com/rpm-definition-what-is-remote-patient-monitoring#:~:text=The%20following%20is%20shared%20on,when%20necessary%2C%20recommendations%20and%20instructions.

RPM CPT Codes (1): Defining RPM CPT codes

RPM CPT CODES

	99453	99454	99457	99458	99091	0054T
HOW OFTEN	Once per patient	Once per month per patient	Once per month per patient	Recommended to NOT exceed 2 units	Once per month per patient	Once per patient
DESCRIPTION	Time spent for initial setup of RPM services	Monthly remote monitoring (supply and use of medical devices)	First 20 min of time spent with patient	Additional treatment time spent (includes the initial 20)	Standalone collection of remote data (30 min)	Computer-assisted surgical procedure with fluoroscopic images
REIMBURSEMENT	$18.84	$48.93	$47.60	$38.68	$56.41	Separately reimbursed
CATEGORY	Category I: Medical Billing	Category I: Medical Billing	Category I: Medical Billing	Category I: Medical Billing	Category II: Reporting Data	Category III: Emerging Tech
ABILITY TO APPLY	Easy	Easy	Easy	Easy	Medium	Hard

Source: https://smartclinix.net/what-are-the-essential-rpm-cpt-codes/#:~:text=However%2C%20specific%20RPM%20CPT%20codes,CPT%2099458%2C%20and%20CPT%209909, https://blog.prevounce.com/quick-guide-remote-patient-monitoring-rpm-cpt-codes-to-know, https://caresimple.com/new-rpm-codes-99091-99453-99454-99457-99458/

RPM CPT Codes (2): Examples of current RPM CPT codes

Smart medical devices transmit patients' health data to clinicians with greater accuracy, allowing a clearer snapshot of their real-time health status. When this patient data is digitally analyzed along with their medical history in the IoMT network, the work of healthcare providers (HCP) can be conducted with better efficiency. An HCP can check a patient's data and history in the network any time it's needed. And fewer in-person visits to the provider's office translate into lower medical costs along with less chance of infection, especially for vulnerable categories of populations affected by severe or chronic diseases.

WEARABLE BIOSENSORS

The wearable biosensors now available for consumers, patients, and providers are small, lightweight, and easy to wear. They're proving to be a remarkably effective tool in the prevention or management of health issues. By enabling HCP to remotely monitor patients' vital signs like heart rate, body temperature, or breathing rate, wearable biosensors are promoting the rise and effectiveness of virtual caregiving. That being the case, wearable biosensors have received FDA approval as a medical device to support the monitoring of hospitalized patients to detect signs of deterioration.

One such sensor was first used at OLVG Hospital in the Netherlands where it was installed in the isolation rooms of patients suspected of COVID who didn't require ventilation. When placed on the chest of these patients, it recorded and transmitted their respiratory rate and heart rate, data considered to be the main indicator of physical deterioration. Other parameters monitored by the wearable biosensor were activity levels and posture.[93] In another study on Cardiac and

---

93 "Philips Launches Next Generation Wearable Biosensor for Early Patient Deterioration Detection, Including Clinical Surveillance for COVID-19," https://www.philips. com/a-w/about/news/archive/standard/news/press/2020/20200526-philips-

Activity Monitoring (CAM), the wearable biosensors were used to monitor patients with multiple sclerosis (MS). The study demonstrated it's feasible to monitor MS patients' status by capturing data indicating their motion, environmental exposure, body temperature, and heart rate.[94]

VIRTUAL CAREGIVING UNITS

Now that many wearable biosensors have FDA approval, *virtual caregiving units* are utilizing this digital health tech to provide patient care more efficiently. With the help of medical wearables and other monitoring technology, some patients can remain at home where HCPs can treat them remotely. This benefits overcrowded hospitals by freeing up bed space for patients who must be treated on site. In 2020, for example, the Royal Prince Alfred (RPA) Hospital in Australia used a virtual caregiving unit to remotely treat patients experiencing COVID-19 symptoms. Patients remained at home but were equipped with armpit patches to track their body temperature and with small pulse oximeter devices on their fingers to measure their heart rate and the oxygen saturation level in their blood. With the help of an application installed on patients' phones, the collected data was sent to HCPs who could intervene when necessary.[95]

The United Arab Emirates has also created virtual clinics offering remote care to treat a variety of medical specialties, ranging from

launches-next-generation-wearable-biosensor-for-early-patient-deterioration-detection-including-clinical-surveillance-for-covid-19.html.

94   Jessica Nye, "Wearable Biosensors Can Quantify, Monitor MS in Clinic and Free-Living Settings," 2021, https://www.neurologyadvisor.com/topics/multiple-sclerosis/wearable-biosensors-can-quantify-monitor-ms-in-clinic-and-free-living-settings/.

95   Lynne Minion, "'Flattening the Curve' with Virtual Care in Australia," June 30, 2020, https://www.healthcareitnews.com/news/europe/flattening-curve-virtual-care-australia.

cardiology and gynecology to pediatrics and mental health. Originally intended as a preventive measure to stop the spread of COVID-19, these virtual units used smart medical devices and integrated AI solutions to provide medical services without the need for face-to-face meetings between patients and doctors. Since healthcare delivered via virtual clinics was more efficient and cost-effective, their use will undoubtedly continue. And it turned out, most patients were more comfortable at home anyway.

Overall, the main advantage of creating and using "virtual wards" or "hospitals without walls" is how they can improve the delivery of long-term care to patients with chronic diseases. No matter how far patients are from a clinic or hospital, virtual care can increase the amount of medical support provided to patients. And thanks to the help of smart medical devices and technology, it also increases the percentage of people getting their health monitored on a regular basis. App-driven smart thermometers, for instance, can be a valuable help—especially for parents whose children experience fever accompanied by other symptoms.

The data collected by these smart thermometers helps parents check for signs indicating disease. They also help assess if a child's condition is severe enough to warrant an ER or urgent care visit so that unnecessary visits can be avoided. To assist further, supporting apps provide treatment insights to parents based on indicators like their child's age and other symptoms. The data is shared with the family doctor or with the pediatrician who can add it to the patient's medical history and/or use it to make treatment recommendations.

ARTIFICIAL PANCREAS SYSTEMS

Automated insulin delivery (AID) devices provide a closed-loop insulin delivery system that represents a major breakthrough for the

8.5 percent of adults affected by diabetes worldwide.[96] Although inno-vative, the device's operating principle is simple. CGMs repeatedly check a person's blood sugar levels at night to determine how much insulin to administer. An insulin pump delivers the required amount and then continues to adjust that amount based on changing sugar levels in the person's bloodstream.

Used in combination with CGMs, AID systems improve the comfort of people suffering from diabetes by saving them from having to repeatedly test their blood sugar with finger-prick tests. But even more importantly, the AID system maintains stable glucose levels, which protect diabetics from the severe health issues that can result from fluctuating glucose levels. The device also leads to cost savings for the entire healthcare system as it reduces the number of specialized diabetic health interventions.

AI-POWERED CHATBOTS

More digital interactions between patients and clinicians are prompting more automation using AI-powered chatbots that sound human. As these "bots" evolve technologically, they're being enlisted to conduct an ever-wider range of medical tasks. Instead of just sched-uling appointments as you might expect, AI and ML now equip bots to recommend treatments and assess symptoms. Some chatbots, using an algorithm based on the way a doctor thinks and works, can exchange texts or instant messages with patients about symptoms and then provide advice and recommendations.

Increasingly sophisticated AI chatbots can even acknowledge the changes in a conversation partner's moods and adjust their answers accordingly. This feature is intentionally designed to help callers

---

96   "Diabetes," World Health Organization, Centers for Disease Control and Prevention, https://www.who.int/news-room/fact-sheets/detail/diabetes.

navigate through difficult times when they're concerned about a medical problem. To give you an idea of how these more advanced chatbots interact, the Centers for Disease Control and Prevention (CDC) hosts an AI-powered chatbot on its website that can assist patients.[97] Smart AI chatbots have proven to be an efficient solution for remote healthcare interactions, and they're here to stay. As they become ever more "humanized" and sophisticated, AI chatbots will play a widening role in the digital transformation of healthcare.

CARE FOR SENIOR PATIENTS

Most senior citizens who don't have a permanent, in-house caretaker will understand the tremendous potential of RPM devices. Many of them are already using the specially designed pendants that can detect a fall and contact help. Now, these older-generation devices are being redesigned as "smarter" versions that can interconnect with other smart devices, such as thermometers or blood pressure monitors, in the IoMT infrastructure. In the future, more of these devices will become all-in-one devices, such as the Polso VSM, able to provide a complete image of a patient's health changes over time.

Some RPM devices have a video function and are designed to actually learn a person's habits and movements. They can alert a designated caregiver if the patient doesn't show any movement or exhibits a modified movement pattern for an unusual period of time. For patients who feel these devices are too invasive from a privacy standpoint, there are alternatives that use audio rather than video monitoring.

---

97 "Symptoms of COVID-19," https://www.cdc.gov/coronavirus/2019-ncov/symptoms-testing/symptoms.html.

SMART INHALERS

As a physician, it's hard to accept the fact that two out of three asthma deaths could be prevented if patients had been prescribed more suitable medication and a customized treatment plan that was reviewed on a regular basis.[98] Because asthma and other respiratory conditions can't be effectively treated without proper monitoring, smart inhalers are being recommended as a solution to this tracking problem. When used with applications installed on patients' phones, these inhalers monitor their medication plans. They provide alerts in visual and/or audio form to remind patients when it's time to take their medication and what dose they should take. These smart inhalers can also instruct patients on how to optimize their inhaling techniques and how to stick to their medication plan. Based on the data collected, the devices send reports to the patients' physicians, who can decide to change or to adjust the existing medication or treatment plan.

MY EXECUTIVE TAKEAWAY

Going forward, the emergence of new digital therapeutics technologies will continue to increase and enhance patients' remote access to medical care. It's already improving the life conditions of those affected by chronic disease, including elders who live alone and those who are more vulnerable to infections. Such universal value should reassure investors that RPM (and the IoMT that makes it possible) is a good investment, promoting the objectives of these primary healthcare stakeholders:

> ➤ **Providers/physicians/clinicians are using this form of DTx because it results in better health outcomes and management**

---

98   Ingrid Torjesen, "Two Thirds of Deaths from Asthma Are Preventable, Confidential Inquiry Finds," *BMJ* 348 (2014): g3108, https://www.bmj.com/content/348/bmj.g3108.full.

of their patient networks today, with the promise of improved prevention of disease tomorrow.

➢ Patients/consumers welcome the way DTx promotes preventive health by giving them more knowledge and control over their own physical status.

➢ Payers are embracing DTx for the double benefit of promoting preventive health among their beneficiaries while also lowering their costs as insurers.

As a health industry entrepreneur and tech pioneer myself, I'm very excited about the exponential way healthcare DTx is building on itself. By using the computational power of AI and ML, patients are being helped in ways that have never been possible in the past. In the next chapter, I'll describe how voice recognition is doing that—going beyond human capability to foster better mental health at a time when it's desperately needed.

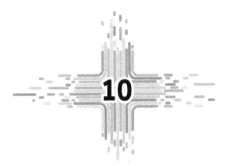

10

THERAPY 2.0

Debugging Mental Health and
Medical Care with Digital Programs

*I'm really excited to see if we can change the paradigm of
mental health and give it some measurement to treat mental
health with the same parity as physical health.*

—GRACE CHANG, FOUNDER/CEO, KINTSUGI

Even before the COVID-19 pandemic of 2020, more than *50 percent* of Americans had experienced a mental illness or disorder at some point in their lifetime.[99] Unfortunately, the pandemic rapidly increased the intensity of societal stressors of all kinds in the form of social distancing, economic insecurity, and fear of contracting the infection itself. A survey conducted by the Kaiser Family Foundation in July 2021 confirmed that expected annual increase, indicating that 53 percent of adults reported mental health issues compared to 32 percent in March of 2021, attributing the increase to COVID-19.[100] Among the negative

---

99   "About Mental Health," Centers for Disease Control and Prevention, https://www.cdc.gov/mentalhealth/learn/index.htm.

100   Liz Hamel, Audrey Kearney, Ashley Kirzinger, Lunna Lopes, Cailey Muñana, and Mollyann Brodie, "KFF Health Tracking Poll: July 2020," KFF, https://www.kff.org/coronavirus-covid-19/report/kff-health-tracking-poll-july-2020.

symptoms experienced were eating difficulties (32 percent), worsening of preexistent chronic affections (12 percent), troubles with sleeping (36 percent), and an increase in substance use and alcohol intake (12 percent).

Although these statistics reveal the increased need for mental health solutions, they come at a time when some in the industry are calling the existing US healthcare system a *sickcare* system. A 2021 global study[101] supports that diagnosis, showing how poorly the US healthcare system compares to those in other high-income countries. It found the top-performing countries overall were Norway, the Netherlands, and Australia. As for the US, it ranked *last*—despite spending far more of its GDP on healthcare than any other country. Surprisingly, US healthcare performed worst in four critical indicators: access to care, administrative efficiency, equity, and healthcare outcomes. It only did well on *measures of care process*, ranking second out of eleven other countries. The good news is that the pandemic's social distancing requirement greatly accelerated better access to mental health support. And it did so by spurring the societal uptake of remote telehealth consultations—a treatment mode many patients now prefer when it comes to receiving mental healthcare. Social distancing also fostered wider use of voice recognition devices, such as Amazon's Alexa, to alleviate loneliness, especially among the elderly.

The uptake of other digital healthcare innovations holds promise too. Besides Alexa, a set of AI apps and online tools have been designed to use ML to track a person's mental status, based on *how* they're speaking. This AI ability empowers providers to use a person's voice as a biomarker to objectively assess their mental health status. It's an

---

101   Eric C. Schneider, Arnav Shah, Michelle M. Doty, Roosa Tikkanen, Katharine Fields, and Reginald D. Williams II, "Mirror, Mirror 2021: Reflecting Poorly," August 4, 2021, https://www.commonwealthfund.org/publications/fund-reports/2021/aug/mirror-mirror-2021-reflecting-poorly?utm_source=linkedin&utm_medium=social&utm_campaign=International+Insights.

amazing voice recognition innovation that holds enormous promise for meeting growing behavioral health needs.

In the past, mental health practitioners were trained to listen carefully to a patient's tone of voice. Now AI is listening too. It's learned to evaluate the way a person's voice sounds when they're experiencing behavioral health changes.

Depressed patients' speech is usually flatter, softer, and more monotone, having more pauses and a reduced pitch range. In contrast, patients with anxiety tend to have tense muscles, speak faster, and have more difficulty breathing. AI detects these vocal changes and others to predict other mental illnesses like schizophrenia and post-traumatic stress disorder. By listening to short video recordings, DL algorithms can uncover additional patterns and characteristics that even trained experts might miss. It's an exciting digital breakthrough for patients and practitioners alike.

One such technology is KiVA, an AI voice biomarker tool developed by the company Kintsugi. The tool helps clinicians detect patients' depression and anxiety more quickly using just their ano-nymized voices. After "listening" to short clips of patients' recorded voices, the AI tool can identify signs of mental health conditions. Instead of using NLP, this technology is based on how patients speak, providing ML models that are uniquely language agnostic.

Kintsugi's CEO, Grace Chang, teamed with ML scientist Rima Seiilova-Olson to found the US startup in 2019. The company has raised $28 million since its inception, but $20 million of that funding came fairly recently in 2022.[102] This Series A funding round was led by

---

102 Heather Landi, "Kintsugi Banks $20M to Scale Up Voice Biomarker-Based Mental Health Tech," March 3, 2022, https://www.fiercehealthcare.com/health-tech/

Insight Partners, a New York–based global venture capital and private equity firm. Seeing how KiVA filled the gap in existing mental health systems, Acrew Capital, Darling Ventures, Citta Capital, Side Door Ventures, Primetime Partners, IT Farm, AngelList Fund, and Alpha Edison joined in. Those additional investors jumped in to fund Kintsugi because they'd identified the need for a voice biomarker that could help clinicians meet growing demand for their mental health services.

According to a global *Lancet* study, incidence of mental health issues is on the rise, but they are only identified by doctors 47.3 percent of the time and noted appropriately 33.6 percent of the time.[103] That means approximately 60–70 percent of people are falling through the cracks. Kintsugi's biomarker tool, KiVA, will help lower those numbers as the company moves forward, working with payers, providers, health systems, and pharmaceutical companies, as well as small- to medium-sized enterprises. It was already adopted by health-care organizations and was on track to be used on millions of patient phone calls by the end of 2022.[104]

THE SMART SPEAKER MARKET IN HEALTHCARE

The popularity of the smart speaker, Alexa, is changing healthcare too. With its ubiquity and usefulness, it's no surprise that the smart speaker market is expected to increase to *$23.3 billion* by 2025 as

---

kintsugi-banks-20m-scale-voice-biomarker-based-mental-health-tech.

103   https://www.thelancet.com/journals/lancet/article/PIIS0140-6736(09)60879-5/fulltext.

104   Alex J Mitchell, Amol Vaze, and Sanjay Rao, "Clinical Diagnosis of Depression in Primary Care: A Meta-Analysis," *Lancet* 374 (2009): 609–619, https://www.fiercehealthcare.com/health-tech/kintsugi-banks-20m-scale-voice-biomarker-based-mental-health-tech.

smart speaker tech and voice user interfaces (VUI) take healthcare into a new digital future of smart, interactive devices.[105]

What makes these speakers "smart" is the ability to reply logically when we talk to them—an ability imparted by their VUI speech recognition technology. VUI understands verbal commands, also known as "intents," and enables the speakers to answer an impressive array of questions. Powered by NLP that's continuously evolving, it's a technology that's intrigued consumers and is being enthusiastically used by young and old alike. In the US alone, nearly *90 million* adults had smart speakers in 2019. Developed by tech giants such as Amazon, Google, Apple, and Microsoft, VUI-driven smart speakers are already changing our daily interactions with these digital devices.[106]

HOW VOICE USER INTERFACES SUPPORT MEDICAL CARE

After Alexa became commonplace in homes, Amazon shifted its focus to the healthcare sector.[107] Other tech giants have gradually done the same, using their technology to improve patient monitoring (either in medical facilities or remotely) in order to ensure patients needing medical help receive it in a timely, appropriate manner. But Alexa developers first had to become compliant with the rules and regulations of the Health Insurance Portability and Accountability Act (HIPAA), protecting the sensitivity of patients' personal health

---

105 "Global Smart Speaker Market Expected to Reach $23,317 Million by 2025," https://www.alliedmarketresearch.com/press-release/smart-speaker-market.html.

106 Bret Kinsella, "Nearly 90 Million U.S. Adults Have Smart Speakers, Adoption Now Exceeds One-Third of Consumers," 2020, https://voicebot.ai/2020/04/28/nearly-90-million-u-s-adults-have-smart-speakers-adoption-now-exceeds-one-third-of-consumers.

107 Eugene Kim and Christina Farr, "Amazon Is Building a 'Health & Wellness' Team within Alexa as It Aims to Upend Health Care," 2018, https://www.cnbc.com/2018/05/10/amazon-is-building-a-health-and-wellness-team-within-alexa.html.

information. Once they'd accomplished that in 2019, Alexa became available to help hospitalized patients. They were able to ask Alexa to perform various tasks—a function made possible by the device's voice connection to Amazon Echo smart speakers.

In recent years, several VUI projects have been implemented to help patients and healthcare professionals in hospital settings. It's a natural fit for patients who can tell the Alexa in their hospital room what they need/want, and the smart speaker program directs the request to the right staff member.

If the patient requests medicine, a nurse receives the notification on her mobile phone. Or a patient can ask Alexa to turn their TV on or off. No matter the type of request, when patients speak it to Alexa and hear the device's vocal response, it seems to diminish the feeling of loneliness some patients experience during hospitalizations.

SMART SPEAKERS CAN MONITOR IRREGULAR HEARTBEATS

Every year, 300,000 people in the US die from suffering a cardiac arrest that occurs outside of a hospital, and scientists are continually searching for solutions to prevent it.[108] In 2019, for example, researchers from the University of Washington (UW) developed a completely nonintrusive smart speaker skill that can detect *agonal*, or gasping, breathing specific to patients in cardiac arrest while they

---

108 Bryan McNally et al., "Out-of-Hospital Cardiac Arrest Surveillance—Cardiac Arrest Registry to Enhance Survival (CARES), United States, October 1, 2005–December 31, 2010," *Morbidity and Mortality Weekly Report. Surveillance Summaries* 60 (2011): 1–19, https://pubmed.ncbi.nlm.nih.gov/21796098.

sleep, without any kind of physical sensor.[109] According to 911 data, 50 percent of those experiencing a cardiac arrest experience this agonal breathing,[110] and once a smart speaker "hears" it, the voice-enabled device can call for help.

Another cardiac study at UW compared intervals between the heartbeats of healthy subjects and hospitalized patients diagnosed with cardiac conditions, such as heart failure. This comparison was made possible with the help of smart speakers that could detect patients' irregular heartbeats. Detecting irregular heartbeats through smart speakers is possible thanks to sonar technology and algorithms that can detect movement of the chest wall and mark the difference between movements caused by breathing and the ones triggered by environmental noise.[111] This tool is regarded by healthcare experts as a future low-cost test tool that can be used frequently and remotely to detect the cardiac arrhythmias that can cause strokes.

ALEXA CREATES VALUE FOR PROVIDERS, PATIENTS, AND CONSUMERS

Medical providers have found Alexa useful too. A 2017 survey of 2,784 physicians revealed nearly one-quarter of them (23 percent) were already using Alexa to save time by performing professional

---

109 Sarah McQuate, "'Alexa, Monitor My Heart': Researchers Develop First Contactless Cardiac Arrest AI System for Smart Speakers," 2019, https://www.washington.edu/news/2019/06/19/first-contactless-cardiac-arrest-ai-system-for-smart-speakers.

110 UW Medicine, "Cardiac-Arrest Detection Developed for Smart Speakers," June 14, 2019, https://newsroom.uw.edu/news-releases/cardiac-arrest-detection-developed-smart-speakers.

111 Anran Wang, Dan Nguyen, Arun R. Sridhar, and Shyamnath Gollakota, "Using Smart Speakers to Contactlessly Monitor Heart Rhythms," *Communications Biology* 4 (2021): 319, https://www.nature.com/articles/s42003-021-01824-9.

tasks completely hands-free.[112] That's still the case. Recording medical notes verbally, for example, helps doctors with their follow-up reports or with drug prescriptions, since humans can speak 150 words per minute but only write 38 words per minute.

The time saved by using Alexa skills enables physicians to see more patients, reduces waiting times in clinics and medical centers, and ultimately saves money throughout the entire healthcare system.

But hands-free note-taking isn't the only benefit Alexa provides to medical staff. Brewster Ambulance Service in Massachusetts has been using Alexa to provide support for Emergency Medical Teams. Alexa can provide real-time information about EMS protocols and correct medical dosages when dealing with urgent cases on-site. By saving precious time, such assistance can mean the difference between life and death.

Alexa can even make diagnostic suggestions with the help of a skill that encompasses emotional intelligence, AI, and DL. After taking into account a patient's age, gender, medication, and other factors, Alexa browses through the expertise and knowledge of more than 107,000 physicians from over 140 specialties before suggesting a potential diagnosis. Moreover, this skill can connect patients with a real physician if further examination is needed. Let's look at some additional examples of Alexa's utility in healthcare settings:

---

112   "Taking the Pulse U.S. 2017," April 2017, https://decisionresourcesgroup.com/report/ttpxus0019-digital-taking-the-pulse-u-s-2017.

Helps Patients Stick to Their Medication Plan

An online Alexa-based application enables nurses, caretakers, and family members to check if a patient has taken their medication, easing caregivers' schedules.

Enables Remote Prescription Refills

With the help of a voice signature, Alexa enables patients to receive prescriptions from a doctor without a face-to-face visit. Pharmacies can also refill patients' prescriptions based on this Alexa skill.

Provides Hospital Information

Alexa can assist users with questions, concerns, or general guidance when a person is being admitted into a hospital. For instance, New Hanover Regional Medical Center (NHRMC) has a skill that can be activated to provide real-time information to anyone going to this medical facility. By simply saying "Alexa, ask NHRMC," patients receive information about any aspect(s) of the hospital including parking, visiting, payment of bills, contact numbers, directions to the hospital, or items needed for a hospital visit..

Prompts First Aid Steps for the Mayo Clinic, initially utilizing Alexa in 2018, meant offering a skill that makes it possible to access hands-free information about how to administer first aid. This skill provides users with instructions for various accidents that require first aid. For example, by simply saying "Alexa, tell Mayo First Aid I need help for a cut," patients will be told how to treat a cut using Mayo's Clinic first aid expertise.[113]

113　Mayo Clinic News Network, "Mayo Clinic Introduces First-Aid Skill for Amazon Alexa," July 23, 2018, https://medicalxpress.com/news/2018-07-mayo-clinic-first-aid-skill-amazon.html.

Promotes Preventive Health Practices

In the case of the Cleveland Clinic, they're using Alexa to provide easy-to-access, voice-based, daily health tips that include everything from remedies for insomnia to the benefits offered by drinking lemon water, activating the entire knowledge base of the Cleveland Clinic.

Explains Healthcare Terminology

Health Care Genius is an Alexa skill that enables users to navigate the complex world of healthcare terminology. By answering questions related to jargon words like "co-pay" or "deductible," this interactive skill is a valuable resource, especially for those looking to better understand how insurance plans work and comparing plan attributes during insurance enrollment periods.

HOW THE DIGITAL HEALTH ECOSYSTEMS CAN HELP

Having acknowledged that health services using digital voice are valuable to the treatment of behavioral health, different stakeholders are taking action to implement it. For payers, that means including virtual behavioral health services in their covered benefits. In response, providers are using integrated platforms that support telemedicine, and big pharma companies are offering digital therapeutics in addition to traditional formulated pills.

The collaborative work of these stakeholders has resulted in an increasingly effective digital health response for the treatment of mental health issues. Use of digital voice optimizes such collaboration; it not only promotes better communication between patients and providers but also improves payers' mental health monitoring abilities to reduce healthcare costs. A Household Pulse Survey published by the

CDC indicates that the stress, social distancing, financial struggles, and loss of jobs associated with mental health issues are estimated to generate additional expenditures of $100 billion to $140 billion for physical and behavioral health services.[114]

Curbing the Rise in Behavioral Health Disorders

After the 2020 COVID-19 pandemic, the CMS facilitated better access to behavioral health services by granting the following emergency waivers:

- **Permission to provide remote treatment for medication-assisted issues**
- **Higher Federal Medical Assistance Percentage rates**
- **Increased reimbursement rates for provided virtual health services and a higher number of eligible suppliers of telehealth services**
- **Relaxation of technology requirements imposed by HIPAA**

These federal waivers should be welcomed by stakeholders ready to implement the benefits of using digital voice to promote mental health. Such implementation is especially timely considering the rapid rise of behavioral health issues in the population. Despite the negative impact of this situation on every healthcare stakeholder, its deleterious effects can be mitigated most effectively by prevention. It's definitely the best solution from a cost-saving and societal-benefit point of view.

Several prevention programs already in place have proved their cost-effectiveness and benefit to patients' mental health status. The *Annual Review of Public Health* has convincingly made the economic

---

114   National Center for Health Statistics. "U.S. Census Bureau, Household Pulse Survey, 2020–2023. Anxiety and Depression," https://www.cdc.gov/nchs/covid19/pulse/mental-health.htm.

case for the prevention of mental illness, showing that programs focused on maternal and newborn mental health, education regarding substance use, and crisis management in mental health have provided ROI of up to $65 per $1 invested.[115] Similarly, high returns have resulted from efforts to increase the awareness of mental health risks by providing customized programs for employees affected by behavioral disorders.[116]

These examples show that policymakers, payers, providers, and employers can turn the tide of negative behavioral health outcomes by working together. Striving for the early prevention of behavioral issues and decreased social stigma of mental health issues are just two of many highly achievable goals.

It's time to leverage the use of data, analytics, and technology like digital voice to promote mental health.

Dynamic data enables healthcare stakeholders to identify the population groups that can benefit most efficiently from customized prevention and treatments such as those using Alexa skills. With the help of advanced analytics, clinical resources can be allocated to the individuals who've been identified as having an increased risk of substance abuse or for developing mental health issues when basic social and economic needs (housing, food, jobs) aren't being met. Combining the use of data and AI enables payers and providers to more accurately project demand for their behavioral health services.

---

115   David McDaid, A-La Park, and Kristian Wahlbeck, "The Economic Case for the Prevention of Mental Illness," *Annual Review of Public Health* 40 (2019): 373–389.

116   "Economic Analysis of Workplace Mental Health Promotion and Mental Disorder Prevention Programs and of Their Potential Contribution to EU Health, Social and Economic Policy Objectives" (Matrix Insight).

MY EXECUTIVE TAKEAWAY

The prevention and treatment of mental health issues with digital voice tools have redefined the healthcare experience for consumers and patients everywhere—including remote patient visits from home to physical visits to the doctor's office to inpatient hospitalizations. Digital voice innovations can alleviate symptoms, help establish diagnosis, and contribute to helping people build healthier lives overall. The digital transformation of healthcare that's given rise to exponential technological innovation is also impacting the rapidly growing field of digital voice tools and applications.

> ➤ Alexa is just one ongoing example of digital voice technology that will continue to evolve, helping optimize the patient–HCP relationship and ultimately improving the delivery of mental health services.

> ➤ Increased consumer receptivity to these types of tools is enlarging the space for innovations providing mental healthcare powered by voice. They can curb the growing epidemic of "deaths of despair" because of suicide from drug or alcohol misuse.

> ➤ Digital voice tools empower those confined to a wheelchair or bed with a sense of control over their environment, providing them the ability to turn on and off the lights or play music through voice commands alone.

> ➤ In the event of emergencies, smart speaker technology like Alexa can call for help or call a patient's relatives when the patient simply needs someone to talk to. Preserving this sense of self-efficacy and control supports mental health when people are feeling most stressed and vulnerable.

Combined efforts of healthcare stakeholders and leaders can foster the accelerated uptake of digital voice solutions to benefit behavioral health. Use of digital voice technology helps eliminate the barriers that deny access to mental health prevention measures and the treatment of behavioral health issues in different populations and diverse geographic locations. As health leaders, we can't afford to look away when digital voice for mental health is already a market-ready solution. So is the direct-to-patient (DTP) healthcare now available from online healthcare platforms that I'll discuss in the chapter ahead.

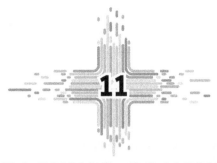

UNLEASHING CONSUMER-DRIVEN HEALTHCARE

Digital Health Solutions
Require Partnering with Providers

While both health systems and technology vendors want to improve shared
successes, neither health systems nor vendors have a comprehensive,
impartial view of all the dynamics and drivers at play on the "other side."

—PAUL TRIGONOPLOS, DIRECTOR, INTERNATIONAL RESEARCH

I have a very personal reason for working to make healthcare more accessible to those who need it. During the last trimester of my first pregnancy, at thirty-eight weeks, I didn't immediately notice my baby had stopped moving. I hurried in to see my obstetrician, but it was too late. Losing my child was devastating. As a physician, I had a hard time dealing with the fact I hadn't detected my baby's loss of movement sooner. How could I have missed it? And what should I have done differently? What *could* I have done? Those questions have fueled my personal and professional resolve to help other women avoid such loss. Working to advance DTP healthcare is one effective way I'm doing that.

Otherwise known as DTC, or on-demand, care, this revolutionary type of healthcare is using digital technology to grant patients/

consumers online access to a growing inventory of the health products and services they need—when they need it. Using online healthcare platforms, healthcare consumers can buy products or services directly without needing to go through a specific payer or provider. But rather than replacing those stakeholders, DTP healthcare is actually creating more opportunity for *all* healthcare stakeholders by offering an additional way to interface with those they serve.

In the case of maternity care, that means an increasing number of women now have access to wearable sensors and devices that monitor both fetal and maternal health to reduce risks during pregnancy. Some of these wearables monitor fetal echocardiography (ECG) (heart rate) and movement, while others focus on the mother's health. That's still a crucial issue since approximately eight hundred women die *daily* from avoidable causes related to pregnancy and childbirth globally.[117] In the US alone, there were 23.8 maternal deaths per 100,000 births in 2020.[118] This is why careful monitoring of vital signs and physical activities is essential to ensuring the mother and fetus's health and safety during pregnancy. Monitoring is often the first step in the early detection of pregnancy abnormalities and risks, but it can also create unnecessary anxiety or over testing. However, I believe being able to track fetal heartbeat and movement in real time might have saved my own baby. That's why it's extremely important to me that patients have access to lifesaving health technology that can track worrisome symptoms, such as early signs of stroke or heart attacks, via RPM.

117   Anika Alim and Masudul H. Imtiaz, "Wearable Sensors for the Monitoring of Maternal Health—A Systematic Review," *Sensors* 23 (2023): 2411, https://www.ncbi.nlm.nih.gov/pmc/articles/PMC10007071/.

118   Maria F. MacDorman, Eugene Declercq, Howard Cabral, and Christine Morton, "Recent Increases in the US Maternal Mortality Rate: Disentangling Trends from Measurement Issues," *Obstetrics and Gynecology* 128 (2016): 447–455. doi: 10.1097/AOG.0000000000001556.

Patient-generated data and current trends suggest that tendency will increase. Telehealth, for example, has been used in the obstetrics field for consultations, ultrasounds, fetal ECG, and postpartum care. More specifically, patients and providers have welcomed the fewer physical obstetric visits in the Mayo Clinic's Obstetric (OB) Nest model, which combines prenatal office visits with virtual visits and in-home monitoring. Studies show the model is actually associated with increased continuity of care and stronger care relationships between pregnant women and their care teams.[119] One study evaluating the OB CareConnect telehealth program found that pregnant women who received virtual care were more satisfied than in-person patients with their care.[120] A randomized trial also found that using telemedicine for patients with low-risk pregnancies saved time and was associated with lower costs.[121]

That makes sense since even a normal, uneventful pregnancy can still pose problems for women using traditional maternity care. Expectant mothers will usually have seven to fourteen in-person obstetrical visits over a nine-month period. Between travel and time issues, making it to those appointments can be difficult. But they're important because prenatal care typically includes nutritional and genetic consultations as well as education about pregnancy, childbearing, breastfeeding, newborn care, and other vital topics.

In addition to offering essential health services, risk assessments, and patient education, those visits are meant to build trust between

---

119 Hameeda Almuslim and Sharifah AlDossary, "Models of Incorporating Telehealth into Obstetric Care During the COVID-19 Pandemic, Its Benefits and Barriers: A Scoping Review," *Telemedicine Journal and E-health* 28 (2022): 24–38, https://www.liebertpub.com/doi/10.1089/tmj.2020.0553#B28; https://www.liebertpub.com/doi/10.1089/tmj.2020.0553#B29.

120 https://www.liebertpub.com/doi/10.1089/tmj.2020.0553#B30.

121 https://www.liebertpub.com/doi/10.1089/tmj.2020.0553#B31.

expectant moms and their providers. So having to miss any or all of them because of work or transportation is a serious issue. It means a woman misses out on important opportunities to monitor and understand her own health and that of her unborn baby. Being able to care remotely with wearable sensors, virtual visits, and the ease of online communication is a win for all stakeholders involved.

NEW MATERNITY HEALTHCARE SOLUTIONS

A few health payers have taken important steps toward supporting and promoting these new types of healthcare solutions. One of those steps was launching a national, value-based reimbursement model for women who had low- to moderate-risk pregnancies. Several other payers followed their example, paving the way to the reimbursement of maternity apps. These apps help equip would-be parents with many of the tools they need:

- Health alerts and reminders
- Option to call a nurse on a twenty-four-hour-a-day basis
- Educational information about maternity
- Resources to access assisted reproductive technology
- Useful advice for managing a high-risk pregnancy
- Cost and quality calculations

Thanks to the competitive nature of innovation, this new direction in digital health tech drove more manufacturers into developing fertility and maternity applications. Some of them went even further. Companies like Wildflower, Maven, Babyscripts, or Ovia created platforms that have provided users with better experiences, services, products, and, most importantly, improved health outcomes. These platforms have merged their design resources in a way that enables a smooth transition from fertility to pregnancy and from pregnancy to maternity by exploring the array of possibilities provided by state-of-the-art technology.

DIGITAL ENGAGEMENT CONTINUUM

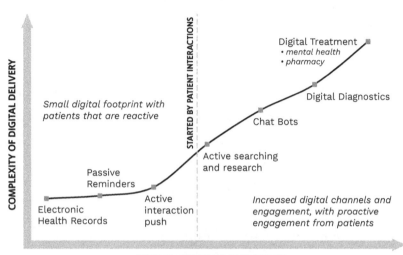

Digital Engagement Continuum: Consumer engagement levels range from passive to active.

The key to these platforms' successes is based on their integrated portfolio of mobile software. Several companies have developed applications that serve the initial purpose of fertility tracking. Once the milestone of conception is achieved, it adjusts to pregnancy by carrying over the information and preferences from the fertility phase into those of pregnancy. Other platforms offer a specialized tool that focuses on supporting the future parent across the entire spectrum of their experiences—through fertility, pregnancy, and the postpartum phase afterward.

Areas of Concern

Since digital maternity and fertility health apps use approximate dates to estimate the ovulating periods of women, several experts in sexual and reproductive healthcare have expressed their confidence that these apps are efficient as long as users understand what they can do and utilize them for the purposes for which they're intended. Although these companies are working to increase the accuracy of results delivered by their apps, it's important to acknowledge and benefit from the complexity of integrated applications already available. There are many to choose from. Some apps provide valuable support to women who want to avoid an unplanned pregnancy, while others support those who want to have a baby. Either way, data generated from the consistent use of these applications is continuously improving them in terms of several key metrics for maternal health: assisted reproductive technology use, C-section percentage, and rates of births that require intensive neonatal care.

These benefits can be used as proof for health payers that their digital maternity and fertility health apps are a solution that can trigger the enrollment of more patients in their plans. Conversely, of course, it will decrease disenrollment from these plans. While the use of these apps can be extremely beneficial, it's important to continue seeing a doctor regularly. A doctor can confirm, through physical examination, that sexual and reproductive health is being preserved.

Direct-to-Consumer Healthcare Is Needed

Of course, greater access to maternity devices and software is just one way that patients are being helped by direct access to health products and services. Consumers' overall satisfaction with virtual care and digital health tech (e.g., wearable sensors) has huge implications for the health industry. I say that because every person will be a patient at some point—which means *everyone* will also be a healthcare consumer. The terms "patient" and "consumer" can be used interchangeably now. Direct access to digital healthcare products and services online has blurred the distinction between the two.

In the future, it's projected that 70 percent of consumers are likely to use digital health solutions, and at least three out of every four consumers believe those solutions would help improve their well-being.[122] This is very good news for a sick healthcare system, as provider shortages increase and healthcare costs rise. That's why it's so transformative that the preventive and potentially lifesaving benefits of digital health tech are now available to consumers directly.

Some providers may cringe at the thought of their patients circumventing legitimate clinical advice and treatment, but that's not how the digital healthcare transformation is unfolding. Healthcare platforms host online consultations/visits with credentialed physicians, nurses, and other certified medical personnel who can order appropriate tests and prescription medications.

In earlier chapters, I described the incredible array of patient and consumer devices now available for the prevention, treatment, and management of chronic disease. Being able to buy these products and also receive medical care and treatment via DTP and DTC is changing healthcare forever. This is the future of health delivery. DTP/DTC has taken the existing availability, affordability, and effectiveness of virtual healthcare and moved it to the next level. It's given savvy consumers and patients exactly what they want: direct, online access to leading-edge HCPs, products, and services via platforms.

From a business perspective, the timing couldn't have been better. Patients and consumers were already taking more interest in managing

---

122   Jessica Hagen, "Q&A: Cost Is the Most Significant Barrier to Digital Health Adoption," March 13, 2023, https://www.mobihealthnews.com/news/qa-cost-most-significant-barrier-digital-health-adoption.

their own health. And it led many of them to search for easier-to-access, less expensive healthcare services. Savvy digital healthcare companies responded by creating online platforms offering DTP/DTC solutions for common health products, devices, and services. This innovation filled a very practical need for a more convenient way to dispense and receive health services. In a healthcare system burdened by chronic disease, costly resources, and burned-out providers, the DTP/DTC solution is a timely one.

It's clear that a growing number of healthcare consumers are no longer willing to cede complete control of their health to a traditional health-delivery system. At the same time, healthcare resources and providers are both being stretched thin. Relying on traditional healthcare alone is no longer a viable option for the patient, provider, and payer stakeholders as costs continue to rise. This combination of factors is driving a DTP/DTC healthcare solution at the time it's most needed.

FACTORS DRIVING CONSUMER HEALTHCARE

In 1970, healthcare spending per person was around $350 annually. By 2019, that cost was $11,582 and a sixfold increase based on the value of a dollar in 2019.[123] One of the most dramatic results of this increase is reflected in younger consumers' approach to healthcare. Because of the expense of health insurance, many of them prefer to pay for it "as needed." They're simply not motivated to pay hundreds of dollars a month for health insurance plans providing services they may not feel they need on a regular basis.

---

123 Liz Kwo, "Direct to Patient Care for Testing and Treating," https://www.everlywell. com/blog/thought-leadership/direct-to-patient-care/.

High Cost of Insurance

For younger healthcare consumers, using DTP/DTC health services fills an existing gap in the industry. They don't mind paying "on the spot" for doctors' visits or occasionally covering tests and meds out of pocket. Of course, that's not a problem for consumers who seldom experience health issues. And DTP/DTC health products and services allow the higher patient involvement younger healthcare consumers prefer. In fact, patients from all age groups have begun to question their doctors about why the medication they've prescribed is necessary or if there are alternatives to a certain medication or treatment. They're also likely to be using wearable health devices and looking for natural alternatives to pharmaceuticals. Even older consumers with Medicare coverage are part of this trend.

Interest in Alternative Medicine

This tendency to try alternative medicine has been triggered, in part, by the proclivity of some doctors to overprescribe medication when it's not really warranted. Increasingly savvy patients/consumers are aware of the mutually beneficial relationship between big pharma and those who benefit from promoting their pharmaceuticals. Like it or not, this suspicion is confirmed by research.[124] One source found that more than 2,500 physicians had received at least half a million dollars apiece from drug makers and medical device companies in a five-year period.[125] Of course, there are many essential medications needed to

---

124 Charles Ornstein, Tracy Weber, and Ryann Grochowski Jones, "We Found over 700 Doctors Who Were Paid More than a Million Dollars by Drug and Medical Device Companies," October 17, 2019, https://www.propublica.org/article/we-found-over-700-doctors-who-were-paid-more-than-a-million-dollars-by-drug-and-medical-device-companies.

125 Mike Tigas, Ryann Grochowski Jones, Charles Ornstein, and Lena Groeger, "Dollars for Docs," October 17, 2019, https://projects.propublica.org/docdollars/.

treat chronic disease, and as of 2021, the World Health Organization (WHO) listed 479 of them. Many of the remaining 20,000-plus pharmaceuticals[126] have been targeted by consumer-advocate campaigns aimed at decreasing the number of prescribed medications that don't provide sufficient benefit to patients.

The Rise of Telemedicine

As you know, telemedicine has several other names, and it isn't really new. It's sometimes called telehealth, e-health, or mHealth (mobile health). But all those terms refer to the same thing: healthcare delivered remotely with technology that transfers digital information between different locations. Although the technology for telemedicine existed prior to the COVID pandemic, its use spiked sharply during that time as HCPs tried to limit the virus's spread through social distancing. Because it was relied upon so heavily, most patients and providers became comfortable using it. And an overall acceptance of all things digital helped pave the way for that receptivity. Now patients and providers routinely expect to enjoy telemedicine's benefits in the form of RPM, patient portals, virtual appointments and visits, personal health applications, and access to the personal health record (PHR) system.

BENEFITS OF DIRECT-TO-PATIENT (DTP) CARE

Typical of iterative innovation, telemedicine's wide acceptance prompted several companies like Everlywell to take the additional step of developing DTP solutions. One of these solutions has given consumers the ability to purchase clinically validated tests directly. Ranging from nutritional health tests to those designed to evaluate

---

126 "FDA at a Glance, " 2023, https://www.fda.gov/about-fda/fda-basics/fact-sheet-fda-glance.

general wellness and sexual health, these tests provide consumers with science-based methods of detecting common health issues more conveniently. These Clinical Laboratory Improvement Amendments (CLIA)[127] and College of American Pathologists (CAP)[128] certified home tests enable patients to find out if they're being affected by any health problem from the comfort of their home—saving the time it would take to make an appointment and go to a laboratory.

Everlywell is one of the companies that has understood how important it is to provide patients with this tool by ensuring the testing methods used have been clinically validated against traditional methods. This process is designed to embed in tests having the same accuracy and reliability expected by patients from any traditional lab work they may use to assess their state of health.

It's an empowering development for patients/consumers because it gives them more control over their health decisions. When a health issue arises, they can access a healthcare platform remotely to find accurate medical information. They'll find details regarding the type of care available, costs involved, expected results of a treatment, how to access that treatment, or how to access a different product or service. These companies enable patients to make informed decisions about how to reach their health goals.

Patients and consumers evaluate DTP healthcare companies based on how easy it is to navigate their online platforms and how readily visitors to the site can locate the company's information, products, and clinical interactions they need. These online health-care companies behave as service providers genuinely interested

127 "Clinical Laboratory Improvement Amendments (CLIA)," CMS.gov, https://www.cms.gov/medicare/quality/clinical-laboratory-improvement-amendments.

128 "Laboratory Accreditation Program," College of American Pathologists, https://www.cap.org/laboratory-improvement/accreditation/laboratory-accreditation-program.

in the welfare of patients and consumers seeking their aid. It's a different, more personal way to offer healthcare. They don't have to operate within payer business constraints or incentives. Instead, they can prioritize partnering with the patients and consumers they're designed to serve—which helps them reach their health goals faster.

THE ADVANTAGES OF DTP HEALTHCARE

The decentralized DTP model is a leading-edge business approach that allows healthcare companies to operate remotely. By freeing telehealth from a single provider, group, or location, it can offer more patients access to high-quality care. This innovative approach leverages existing technology to standardize the healthcare experience by offering it exclusively online. Like traditional telemedicine, DTP care includes consultations, asynchronous messaging with health providers, and RPM. An additional advantage of this model is that it offers at-home testing. Even so, the most important aspect of DTP is the way it puts healthcare at patients' fingertips in a very literal sense—via any device connected to the internet. Instead of forcing patients to spend time randomly searching for a provider, it offers patients a centralized, user-friendly interface throughout the US. Like so many other internet conveniences it affords, DTP companies offer improved access to health providers and their services.

DTP companies have a more patient-centric business model that allows them to maximize every dollar spent on their healthcare products and services. They do this by avoiding the enormous cost of "brick-and-mortar" facilities that limit their patient base. Instead, they invest their resources in accredited medical experts, products, and testing services. This strategy enables them to optimize their ability to meet patients' specific demands—no matter where they live.

DIGITAL HEALTHCARE PLATFORM PROVIDES CONSUMERS ACCESS TO AN OPEN INTEGRATED HEALTH ECOSYSTEM

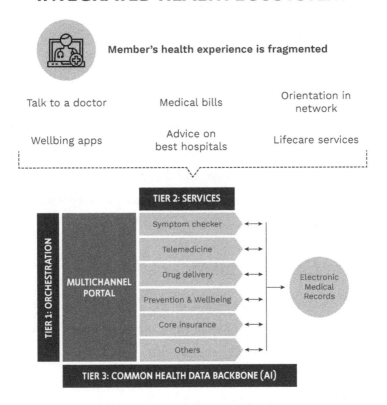

Digital Healthcare Platforms: This digital technology is reducing healthcare costs while offering accelerated remote patient support and virtual care.

Grants Optimal Convenience

Online DTP healthcare is a welcome alternative for patients seeking local providers who may (or may not be) accepting new patients. Even those with standard insurance will have to navigate their insurer's portal to try to find someone in their area that's in network. Even when they do, they have no way of knowing if that provider is good or bad without visiting other websites to look for external reviews (which are spotty, at best). And another problem is that those insurance portals usually advise users to call the provider's office to verify they're *still* actually in network.

Even after all these steps and successfully making an appointment, actually getting to see a provider can still take weeks of waiting even if a patient simply wants the doctor or nurse practitioner to order a test or prescribe medicine for a common ailment like a urinary tract infection. A physical, in-person visit may mean taking time off (maybe unpaid) from work, arranging childcare, and then repeating the process if a follow-up is needed. Another reason is that patients assume the cost will be too high, and they might not be able to afford it in their budget. As a result, these difficulties can keep patients from seeing a doctor or taking care of their health properly.

Provides Cost Transparency

Lack of cost transparency is one of the biggest challenges within the traditional healthcare model. The patient isn't privy to knowing the full cost of their care nor the portion of the cost they're responsible to pay. In fact, many patients are uncomfortable even asking the question! That's quite strange when you stop to think about it. Every other consumer service either advertises what it's going to cost or assumes a customer will ask. Imagine not knowing the price of something when you purchase the service.

Getting sick and requiring healthcare in America is something like getting stranded after your car breaks down and needing help but not knowing the cost of the tow truck or the repair bill. If that's not disclosed (by any service provider) until after the work is done, there's no way to compare quality or the price of services beforehand. And since you need your car, you have no choice but to pay for it. DTP healthcare helps solve that problem by allowing patients to purchase care directly from healthcare companies who are much more transparent about the cost of their care and treatment and any out-of-pocket costs patients incur.

Creates a Universal Access Point

Companies who've invested in DTP care are optimizing the use of existing technology to create a more universal access point to high-quality care for their patients. And they're doing that without bypassing providers. The DTP approach functions as a virtual liaison between health providers and patients similar to the way conventional telemedicine does. Although DTP companies can partner with insurers, they also provide direct healthcare access for uninsured patients. It offers those patients a more cost-transparent, convenient form of telemedicine that may meet their needs better than location-based providers can. That being said, DTP companies must work in tandem with local health providers who will need to see patients in person for all but their most common health problems. This mutually beneficial collaboration will free local providers from the routine health concerns that DTP healthcare is set up to address.

Offers Consumer Choice

Consumers want to know their choices and compare those choices based on cost and quality. In the past, healthcare hasn't made that possible. One patient of mine told me they'd had to visit different hospitals to ask the price of a surgery they needed. The cost varied by tens of thousands of dollars from one facility to another. CMS is addressing that issue by requiring hospitals to disclose the cost of hundreds of their most common procedures or face penalties. It's a very hopeful sign that healthcare is shifting toward a more consumer-friendly model that provides cost transparency for acute care.

For non-acute care, DTP companies are beating out traditional providers by offering price and quality transparency for its consults, products, and testing. Every person who's sought health services knows this isn't yet available with traditional healthcare delivery. The cost of their health services isn't advertised—whether it's a consult, lab work, or a medical device that's needed.

> **Although providers may complain about patients who come to see them after they've consulted "Dr. Google," those patients are simply doing what savvy consumers do: they seek information so that they can make informed decisions.**

The days of treating clinicians as gods who know everything are long gone (except among the elderly). Even the millions of US baby boomers who are aging into the need for more health services don't want to leave their brains at the door. That old-school mindset is particularly onerous to younger consumers who tend to question *everything*. They know how to scour the internet for information and services that give them what they're looking for at the lowest cost and greatest convenience. It's what they've come to expect in every aspect of their lives, and healthcare is no different now.

Supports Uninsured Patients

Because healthcare is expensive, some patients are forced to give up other essentials to take care of their health. That may mean they can't afford to take their prescribed medication(s), or they may skip going to the doctor when they're not feeling well. Even though public programs like Medicaid and the ACA exist to serve lower-income individuals, some patients aren't "poor enough" to participate, and they may still find individual market plans expensive. DTP health-care can help provide access to limited forms of care—with known cost—to individuals who might otherwise delay care to pay for other essentials in their budget.

CHALLENGES OF DIRECT-TO-PATIENT CARE

As with any newcomer to the healthcare system, DTP companies face challenges. The most significant issue is maintaining the privacy of user data. It's a familiar problem across the transforming landscape of digital health services. Today's consumers are more informed than ever and are aware of the risk that data collected from them may be exposed by mistake or be illegally exploited and sold. Understandably, it makes patients more reluctant to share their personal data.

According to a report published in 2019, 73 percent of respon-dents declared they were willing to share data with physicians, but only 10 percent will do so with tech companies and only 19 percent with pharmaceutical companies.[129] And in 2022, survey respondents reported much higher rates of trust in doctors/clinicians (77 percent) compared to other sources outside of the formal healthcare system, including digital health apps (28 percent), websites (16 percent), and social media groups (11 percent).[130]

For health-tech companies who need data to create more person-alized products and services, this patient reluctance represents a serious obstacle. Without trust, consumers (patients, in this case) won't want to share their data, especially with new companies offering health-care online via telemedicine. This means those new companies must

---

129   Kwo, "Direct to Patient Care for Testing and Treating."

130   Madelyn Knowle, Adriana Krasniansky, and Ashwini Nagappan, "Consumer Adoption of Digital Health in 2022: Moving at the Speed of Trust," February 21, 2023, https://rockhealth.com/insights/consumer-adoption-of-digital-health-in-2022-moving-at-the-speed-of-trust/.

commit to making an all-out effort to ensure data security in order to gain patient and consumer trust. Once they've met that objective, they'll need to publicize it using customized marketing techniques and e-commerce strategies.

One excellent strategy is enabling customers and potential customers to publish product and service reviews. This will require asking patients questions about their experience using a DTP platform and publishing their answers on the site. As in other industries, it's one of the least expensive and effective methods of proving the platform's validity and building a relationship of trust with its customers. Another proven method is to deliver products and services of high standard and quality. This ensures the consumers will feel comfortable sharing their user experience in a way that helps define and grow the reputation of DTP companies' products and services.

By using notifications, for example, a DTP company such as Everlywell can alert individual consumers to new products and services or those that are most appropriate for them. This type of personalized approach is one that online consumers have come to expect in recent years. It's the new normal online, and it provides these consumer-facing companies with the opportunity to stand out by exceeding expectations with FDA-approved health solutions, which are more affordable and convenient. As consumers become patients on DTP platforms, the companies who can prove they're providing reliable data protection will gain patients' trust and build the good reputation that generates consumer confidence.

MY EXECUTIVE TAKEAWAY

DTP care is here to stay. That being the case, it's a given that competition in the DTP health space will grow rapidly as this form of health delivery expands into its market potential—and that's a good thing.

As these telehealth companies push forward to excel, more consumers and patients will be able to benefit from the products and services their DTP healthcare approach provides. If you've founded one of those companies, or represent one, you undoubtedly already know it requires a lot of effort to build a DTP company that remains true to a strong patient focus:

➢ Keeping tabs on the pulse of how the market is changing

➢ Overcoming obstacles created by other players in the healthcare industry

➢ Constantly innovating and iterating on your products and services

The incomparable power of e-commerce is that it has the potential to reach consumers almost anywhere in the world. This provides DTP companies with the powerful opportunity to deliver their home-use tests and treatment products directly to customers, without needing to rely on any middlemen. Once established, companies offering telehealth can use this direct connection to establish an ongoing relationship with consumers.

A DTP company can educate consumers with valuable health information, provide consults with clinicians, and offer the recommended at-home tests and products patients can purchase directly on the platform.

The DTP healthcare delivery approach is uniquely accessible, with the ability to open and maintain a 24/7 communication link with their customers. When it comes to healthcare services, consumers value this connection in case their health needs change. I'm excited to see how this market matures and which of your health solutions emerge to take advantage of this opportunity to deliver value to patients.

CONCLUSION:
THE FUTURE IS NOW

Digital health technology is constantly improving the diagnosis and treatment of disease with new testing techniques. Cagri Savran's work developing a new application of liquid biopsy to detect breast cancer is a good case in point. This is just one of the technologies that will fuel innovation among the millions that can succeed with the key stakeholders aligned. In writing this book, I wanted to take an example of one innovation and summarize learnings into a succinct way to review the healthcare ecosystem. We will zoom in on this technology in this final chapter to summarize the past few chapter learnings and then zoom out as we discuss the future of digital health in the various applications as it is analyzed by payers.

While working with his research team at the Birck Nanotechnology Center in Purdue's Discovery Park, Cagri Savran achieved the breakthrough he was hoping for. The Purdue University mechanical engineering professor was able to create a novel liquid biopsy device that could detect a particularly aggressive, recurrent form of triple negative breast cancer (TNBC). Even after successful cancer treatment via chemotherapy and surgery, patients with TNBC battle fear of its recurrence. The cancer is so likely to recur that patients may fear every headache or back pain indicates their cancer is coming back. Savran's novel use of liquid biopsy has offered a noninvasive way to reassure those patients and their physicians about their remission status.

The trial proved that genetic and cellular material from tumors find their way into a patient's bloodstream in the form of tumor DNA (ctDNA) and circulating tumor cells (CTC).[131] These CTC cells are so rare that there may only be three or four out of the billions of cells in an eight-milliliter blood sample. By detecting cancer cells earlier, the device made it possible to treat TNBC more cheaply and effectively.

> **Cost of use is one of the biggest hurdles faced by startups looking for ways to have their new solution covered. So are scalability and versatility.**

The fact that Savran's device relied on liquid biopsy made it attractive to established healthcare companies. Using it to detect cancer would be cheaper than surgical biopsy. Savran's novel microfluidic platform passed the tests of scalability and versatility too. It makes CTC detection so simple and rapid that it will be applicable to other forms of cancer as well.

PAYER REIMBURSEMENT IS KEY TO INNOVATION

Liquid biopsy is just one way digital health tech is continuing to revolutionize medicine as iterative innovation accelerates. Despite this momentum, there are some major hurdles to overcome. To succeed in the long term, anyone who owns a digital health company or plans to start one needs to understand how the healthcare system works. *Failure*

---

131 "Liquid Biopsy Tech Contributes to Successful Clinical Trial for Detecting Breast Cancer Recurrence," News release, Purdue University, July 27, 2020, accessed August 4, 2020. https://bit.ly/2D9JMIH.

to identify and navigate its barriers is the reason so few startups offering brilliant healthcare innovations survive. Running a drug manufacturing startup, or any other kind of company in the health space, means identifying who the main players are. And it's equally crucial to *comprehend the established relationships between those various healthcare stakeholders.*

Still, the biggest hurdle, both during and after development, is knowing how you can convince payers to reimburse the product or service you provide. That means your business plan or project argumentation needs to show *how a payer or an employer will benefit from agreeing to cover the cost of adopting your product or service innovation.* This being the case, it's absolutely essential that entrepreneurs have the *tools, endurance, knowledge,* and *value levers* in place to turn an idea into a reimbursed product or service. To succeed, they must anticipate being able to go the distance on what will be a very long journey. I'll use the development of liquid biopsies as an example to illustrate this point and discuss representative challenges.

Coverage Challenges: The Liquid Biopsy Example

A study on private payer and Medicare coverage for circulating tumor DNA testing revealed some of the obstacles to getting public and private payers to cover liquid biopsies.[132] The study and its authors identified the following impediments:

- Individual policies limit coverage to certain clinical scenarios and use overly strict definitions that are written for single-gene analysis or for specific test brands.

---

132 Michael P. Douglas, Stacy W. Gray, and Kathryn A. Phillips, "Private Payer and Medicare Coverage for Circulating Tumor DNA Testing: A Historical Analysis of Coverage Policies From 2015 to 2019," *Journal of the National Comprehensive Cancer Network* 18 (2020): 866–872, https://pubmed.ncbi.nlm.nih.gov/32634780/.

- There are differences between what tests actually measure, what a payer is willing to cover, and what information clinicians receive and can use to guide medical decisions.

- Prior authorization requirements for clinicians delay or prevent patients' access to testing.

Generally, individual payers have complex coverage policy decision protocols that make their coverage policies difficult to readily understand. One payer may approve and cover several types of tests, another may reimburse only for basic tests, and others may restrict coverage to only testing for certain, highly specific genes and clinical conditions. This makes it difficult to evaluate and track existing policies providing coverage. It also causes newcomers to the liquid biopsy market to take longer to understand how things work and how they should position their products to qualify them for coverage. Herein lies the advantage of certain pioneers able to create a moat.

Guidelines for Liquid Biopsy Adoption

At the other end of the decision-making spectrum, any presentation to top payer executives proposing coverage for liquid biopsy tests for cancer screening needs to answer these two questions:

1. Which criteria should be used to assess the use of liquid biopsies for insurance medicine?

   □ *Analytical validity* determines if test results are identical, reproducible, and reliable when sent to four different laboratories.

   □ *Clinical validity* proves prognostic value of the test or that it helps establish a patient will develop an impairment without it.

- *Clinical utility* shows test results are actionable and can be used as a logical basis for impacting decisions that will improve patients' health outcomes.

2. What evidence should manufacturers present to a health insurer considering whether a certain liquid biopsy solution is appropriate for coverage?

- *Sensitivity-level evidence:* The level of false negatives and false positives can lead to patient misdiagnosis and unnecessary treatments.

- *Circulating material evidence:* Low levels of cancer cell indicators in blood samples negatively impact researchers, providers, and insurers since test results are unreliable.

These two issues negatively impact not only market revenue for liquid biopsies but the revenue of health insurance companies as well. This is why it's so important that manufacturers prove their tests can improve *clinical outcomes* (e.g., a decrease in mortality as a result of early cancer detection) and *economic outcomes* too (less effective therapeutics are no longer necessary and reduce expenditures). Liquid biopsy manufacturers/vendors should also provide health insurance companies with information about any projected research delays for tests, regulatory obstacles, or reduced purchase from healthcare providers. Manufacturers/vendors also need to inform payers about potential macroeconomic challenges and their impact on the test's production, approval, and utilization process. The following important factors need to be taken into account when considering creating value for insurance companies.

REDUCED COSTS OR HIGHER REVENUES

Understanding what payers care about isn't complicated. A digital health or drug manufacturing company that's trying to convince a payer to agree to cover their products or services only needs to focus on two things: either reduce payers' costs or increase their revenues. Even better, do *both*. Tech pioneers need to show payers how their solution can satisfy those two value levers in the following ways:

> ➤ *Payers' costs can be reduced by decreasing administrative costs* (cuts their labor costs), *improving cost of care* (reduces medical costs spent on members), and *reducing drug costs* (saves money spent on members' prescriptions).

> ➤ *Payers' revenues can be increased by boosting membership, lowering membership disenrollment, and closing care gaps so that the government reimburses at a higher rate.*

Decreasing Payers' Administrative Costs

Digital health entrepreneurs need to have a comprehensive understanding of the specific ways they can help payers reduce their administrative costs. Armed with those insights, tech pioneers can show how their innovations strategically solve payers' administrative problems with the following solutions.

1. Solutions for Sending Claims Attachments in an Electronic Format

Problem: Since claims attachments are different kinds of documents that accompany patients' health insurance claims, they obviously need to stay with the claim. But that doesn't always happen, and it's a problem that slows down the entire process for everyone. This documentation "backs up" the claim in various ways and can include the notes clinicians take during patient consultations as well as discharge letters, medical certificates, and operative reports. I probably don't need to point out that there are vast troves of these documents and that sending them manually via email or fax doesn't just risk their loss but is also more time-consuming.

Even so, the Council for Affordable Quality Healthcare® (CAQH) index[133] indicates that an astonishing 70 percent of claims attachments continue to be sent via email or fax. And that was the case despite the fact that 96 percent of healthcare claims (as opposed to claims attachments) from health providers were being submitted electronically. Processing the medical attachments manually increases payers' administrative burdens and costs, since employees, such as customer service representatives, must sometimes check the same documents being received several times. But requiring the electronic submission of medical claims attachments is not yet a reality because there is no federal provision to regulate it.

Solution: This is where a digital health company can intervene and add value for payers. Tech pioneers can propose (and facilitate) alternative ways for payers to deal with the random nature of claims attachments submitted manually. A secure web portal shared by medical providers and payers can streamline the process. It can enable the creation of real-time requests for medical claims attachments when an insurance claim is actually submitted, *before* the authorization process begins. This type of solution is just one example of how a digital health or IT healthcare company can seek reimbursement status by suggesting a solution their company provides, that is, a secured web portal.

---

133 Council for Affordable Quality Healthcare, "CAQH CORE Attachments: Health Care Claims Data Content Rule," v. HC.1.0, April 2022, https://www.caqh.org/sites/default/files/CAQH%20CORE%20Attachments%20Claims%20Data%20Content%20Rule%20vHC.1.0.pdf.

2. Options for Streamlining Medical Providers' Authorization Process

Problem: Ask any payer or provider, and they'll agree that the prior authorizations required from insurance companies before they'll approve the cost of patients' medical treatments have increased, and it's a huge problem. That's confirmed by an American Medical Association (AMA) survey,[134] reporting that 88 percent of physicians said burdens associated with prior authorization were "high" or "extremely high." This costly administrative burden pulled resources from direct patient care when providers had to complete an average of forty-five prior authorizations per physician, per week, according to the AMA. Doing so consumed fourteen hours, almost two business days of physician and staff time.[135] Part of the problem is that many health providers still complete these requests either by fax or by phone instead of electronically. And that's the case despite HIPAA Healthcare Service Review X12-278 that regulates the electronic submission of prior authorization requests. Prior authorizations conducted via fax or phone take nearly double the time, requiring about sixteen minutes to complete, as opposed to the estimated nine minutes required to complete a prior authorization electronically. Full adoption of the electronic authorization process by health providers would save $7.28 per transaction.[136]

---

134   Kevin B. O'Reilly, "7 Prior Authorization Terms That Drive Every Doctor to Distraction," November 13, 2023, https://www.ama-assn.org/practice-management/prior-authorization/7-prior-authorization-terms-drive-every-doctor-distraction.

135   "Toll from Prior Authorization Exceeds Alleged Benefits, Say Physicians," March 13, 2023, AMA, https://www.ama-assn.org/press-center/press-releases/toll-prior-authorization-exceeds-alleged-benefits-say-physicians.

136   "2018 CAQH Index," CAQH, https://www.caqh.org/sites/default/files/explorations/index/report/2018-index-report.pdf.

Solution: Digital tech startups can provide value to health systems with innovative solutions that make the prior authorization process more efficient.

One solution, for example, improves precision medicine specialty authorizations by providing a digital access point via telephone so that genetic specialists and physicians can consult regarding the necessity of a specific genetic test. This solution offers a dual benefit by decreasing payers' administrative costs while also reducing the expense of unnecessary genetic tests conducted for patients who could benefit from a different type of testing—as indicated by their individual medical needs and medical history.

3. Improve Cost of Care to Reduce Medical Costs Spent on Members

Problem: Everyone working in healthcare knows the *cost of care* (COC) is rising rapidly. According to CMS, the National Health Service's (NHS) spending is projected to increase annually to reaching $6.2 trillion by 2028.[137]

Solution: Since rising healthcare costs are impacting all stakeholders, it's no surprise many digital health entrepreneurs and companies are working overtime to create solutions that decrease COC. Some that have already been implemented include companies (e.g., Aver) that have simplified the shift from the traditional fee-for-service reimbursement models to VBC contracts with CMS-certified platforms. Offering specialized software products and expertise in alternative payment methods, these platforms allow payers to create and implement VBC contracts. Payers also have access to end-to-end administrative tools, such as claims adjudication, audit reporting, or reconciliation.

---

137   "National Health Expenditure Projections 2019–2028," cms.gov, https://www.cms.gov/files/document/nhe-projections-2019-2028-forecast-summary.pdf.

AI platforms like the one designed by Hindsait can also track biases, human errors, and anomalies in a way that enables payers and other healthcare stakeholders to eliminate abuse, unneeded health services, and waste. Other startups have also focused their attention on customizing *automated patient billing*, providing billing teams with tools that allow them to manage the billing process more effectively. Inbox Health, for example, has developed a platform that integrates algorithms customized to individual practices' needs and to each patient at those practices. It facilitates a two-way communication between a practice and a patient with the help of email, SMS, voice technology, and regular postal mail.

Additional companies such as iShare Medical have used AI and ML to create online platforms that monitor, analyze, and predict what happens within the health system itself. The platform provides secure sharing of medical information and is able to provide feedback that improves the accuracy of existing predictive models. This gives health providers reliable information they can use to improve their medical decision process. Providers are better able to track, prevent, and treat diseases at an earlier stage, which improves the COC and payers' spending on their members.

4. Lower Members' Drug Costs to Reduce Money Spent on Members

Problem: Like other aspects of healthcare, prescription drug prices continue to rise. Because chronic disease has reached epidemic proportions in the US, the cost of medicine is negatively impacting most stakeholders. Payers, in particular, are actively seeking ways to reduce that expense and decrease what they spend for their members' prescription drugs. Digital health startups and established healthcare companies have taken on the challenge in a variety of innovative ways:

Solution: Using AI-driven platforms and mutually beneficial stakeholder collaborations, digital healthcare companies are already providing timely solutions. Equipped with an AI engine, the Benjamin platform, as an example, helps patients manage their medications more efficiently and is able to lower their costs by checking the market to find the best price for their prescription drugs. What makes the platform uniquely effective is that their price search takes the variable of each patient's health insurance status into account, including their coverage and deductibles, out-of-pocket costs, and copays. Drug costs are also reduced thanks to the way the platform's clinicians are using telehealth to discuss the best and most cost-efficient medication with the members of different payers.

SwiftRx is another innovative solution using an integrated technology developed by RxRevu to allow health providers to see prior authorizations. Providers can also access real-time information about a patient's drug options as per their benefit data. This cooperation between health insurers and pharmacy benefits managers (PBMs) allows the provider to make the best decision in terms of the medication selected and provided. Such technology drives the selection of lower-cost options and translates those selections into cost savings for health systems that have pharmacy-fulfillment options.

5. Convince Payers to Cover Gene and Cell Therapy

Problem: Gene and cell therapies (also known as regenerative medicine) aim to correct or replace patients' abnormal genes or cells to restore their normal functions. By regenerating or restoring cells and tissues, genes that don't perform normally, for example, can be modified to help the body fight against different genetic diseases.

Solution: The difference between the two therapies is that *gene therapy replaces a faulty gene*, whereas *cell therapy transfers healthy cells into the body to help treat or cure the disease.* Also known as genome editing, gene therapies can be conducted either inside a patient (in vivo) or outside a patient (ex vivo). This therapy impacts patients' health outcomes in several ways:

Researchers are looking for ways to use gene and cell therapy to treat severe illnesses, such as cancer, hemophilia, heart disease, cystic fibrosis, diabetes, and AIDS. The approach has already shown some success addressing diseases like leukemia, severe combined immunodeficiency, blindness caused by retinitis pigmentosa, and hemophilia. Many other gene and cell therapies are currently in development for rare diseases that lack alternative treatment options. Since gene therapy has been able to correct faulty genes with a single administration, it's a very active area of research.

Payers regard gene and cell therapy as a "shock claim" because *the treatment is only applied one time and has extremely high costs*—unlike the majority of traditional cures. Instead of paying the cost of gene and cell therapy treatments over an agreed-upon period of time, the "sponsor" needs to take in the whole cost in a single tranche. *That's an issue, since the cost of cell therapies average close to $500,000. And the price tag can go even higher, with one gene therapy costing $1 million.*[138]

A digital health company that proposes such an expensive therapy to a health payer must also present solutions for managing the budgeting and stop-loss challenges this therapy would entail.

It's essential to create and propose new reimbursement models that could address the high costs of gene and cell therapy efficiently while also preserving patients' access to the care they need.

---

138 Genetic Engineering and Biotechnology News, "Cell and Gene Therapy Manufacturing Costs Limiting Access," February 21, 2023, https://www.genengnews.com/insights/cell-and-gene-therapy-manufacturing-costs-limiting-access/.

The main argument is that these therapies will be cost-effective in patient illness where a rapid cure will replace years of costly treatments. That being the case, it's still true that the *disorders and diseases targeted by gene and cell therapies don't occur frequently.* Rare forms of cancer or rare genetic deviations are good examples. The takeaway here is that a payer's risk of having to face this type of claim is low. Even so, gene and cell therapy solutions are a rising trend.

Some experts predict that the majority of drug manufacturers will focus on more common health afflictions, such as heart failure or HIV, which would lead to an increase in people eligible for gene and cell therapies. Payers who choose to develop plans for addressing these future changes will be the ones best prepared to absorb the costs of the future gene and cell therapy solutions.

One of the strategies for handling these future cost challenges is to use outcomes-based reimbursement. Because it links reimbursement to the success of therapy, it will still permit compensation even if the therapy fails. But as in the case of other high-cost treatments, there is no fit-to-all solution. Instead, digital health companies and entrepreneurs should be actively developing and should be involved in relationships between manufacturers, payers, and HCPs.

6. Help Payers Prevent Membership Disenrollment

Problem: In the US healthcare marketplace, many health payers compete to gain employment-based insurance contracts and individual memberships. What's more, each participant can change the way they participate. Insured members, for example, can switch their insurers as can employers and move from one payer to another if they choose. Not only that, Medicare and Medicaid members can disenroll from these plans and enroll in privatized plans instead. All of this fluidity impacts health insurers in a big way, whether they're public or private, and it's an element important enough to require identifying the main causes for patients' disenrollment.

To cope with this instability, CMS ruled that patients enrolled in Medicare Advantage plans needed to stay enrolled for at least a quarter before being permitted to switch their health insurer. CMS argued the change was needed to enable health payers to have a predictable membership base. That way, they could invest more heavily in preventive care and provide their members with more benefits. This "lock-in" period also gave members more time to understand the benefits of the plans they were enrolled in. As a result of CMS's decision, the following insights were revealed:[139]

- **Disenrolling is the tool members use to express dissatisfaction with their health plans or health insurers.**

- **Limiting members' options to leave insurance plans "at will" causes inconveniences for them, but it also causes health insurers to improve the services they provide to their enrolled members.**

Some studies have established that there's a direct connection between annual disenrollment rates and a health payer's poor performance.[140] As a result, disenrollment rates can be used as an indicator of a health plan's quality—one that's understood by both payers and patients. These studies also revealed that patients who decide to leave a health plan do so for logical reasons rather than emotional ones. And they only leave after experiencing situations in which the health plan failed to meet their needs or expectations.

---

139 Mary Laschober, "Mathematica Policy Research," *Health Care Financing Review* 26, no. 3 (Spring 2005).

140 Chartis, "In a Shifting Market, Medicare Advantage Shows Continued Growth," March 23, 2023, https://www.chartis.com/insights/shifting-market-medicare-advantage-shows-continued-growth.

Solution: That "failure gap" is the exact place digital health companies and entrepreneurs want to play in. By play, I mean *innovate*. It's where they'll be able to identify how to provide members with the services, products, and tools that most consumers value in their health plans and health insurers. And, of course, having that information will help payers decrease member disenrollment. On the flip side, digital health startups rely on health insurance applications as a fast, handy, and easy-to-access list of solutions indicating what's important to patients.

Fertility Health Apps

Fertility apps, for example, are a digital experience designed to "speak" the language of their users. In most cases, these apps are integrated solutions that support future parents in their journey to parenthood. They keep track of women's menstrual cycles and collect data that enables specialists to establish if they are fertile or not. When the data is correctly and consistently entered in the app, some of these apps can estimate fertile days—information which is very useful for women who want to have a baby. Moreover, some of the apps' developers have quickly understood the diversity of the families looking to have a baby and have adapted their products to modern family structures, such as LBGTQ+ or single-parent families.

Musculoskeletal Health Apps

Another example of applications adopted in recent years by HCPs and patients are musculoskeletal-focused digital apps (MDAs). These apps are being used for pain management, treatment of musculoskeletal disorders, and behavioral health as well.

Musculoskeletal (MSK) disorders, conditions, and injuries increase insurance costs for employers and translate into more lost workdays than any other chronic condition. More than a decade ago, half of all adults in the US had been diagnosed with an MSK condition. [141]

Yet, the majority of those patients weren't benefiting from evidence-based care but being inadequately treated with analgesics and surgery. In fact, those surgeries and other medical costs associated with MSK disorders are more than $20 billion annually.[142] The good news is that much of this costly intervention can be avoided with physical therapy and other noninvasive recovery techniques like those provided by MDAs.

As a result, the number of mobile health apps addressing MSK conditions and injuries has increased rapidly as more health and wellness companies have become interested in the pain management of MSK issues. It's been a smart move since MDAs can provide the following needed benefits:

- Create powerful connections between the mind and the body to help alleviate pain

- Promote mindfulness practice and physical or mental exercise programs

- Monitor pain and the progress of a patient's therapy with sensors applied to body areas affected by MSK disorders

---

141 Stuart I. Weinstein and Edward H. Yelin, "Lost Work Days," Bone and Joint Burden, https://www.boneandjointburden.org/fourth-edition/id2/lost-work-days.

142 Matthew Gavidia, "Hinge Health: Musculoskeletal Costs Doubled in Past Decade with No Benefit in Patient Outcomes," March 26, 2021, https://www.ajmc.com/view/hinge-health-musculoskeletal-costs-doubled-in-past-decade-with-no-benefit-in-patient-outcomes.

- Provide users with access to a library containing exercises designed to prevent MSK episodes through stretching, yoga, Pilates, and many more types of exercises

Companies have even created special MDAs to support postoperative pain management. With their ability to monitor patients' postoperative pain and symptoms in real time, these MDAs are designed to distract patients from focusing on their pain. And these devices are getting ever more sophisticated and customized as AI-powered solutions create more advanced iterations. MDAs are a good example of how digital health technologies are transforming healthcare as they speed up the evolution of innovation in every area of health-tech development.

THE FUTURE OF HEALTHCARE BELONGS TO THE PIONEERS

The steady winds of digital change are blowing in the US healthcare system. Digital health companies and entrepreneurs can take advantage of these fair winds to propel them forward through the process of securing reimbursement for their health-tech solutions. Health payers are eager to see how those solutions can decrease their expenses and/or increase their revenues. Of course, they'll want to see those specifics spelled out by strategic, well-prepared pioneers who know how to build their business cases with data, facts, and figures. Many brilliant health-tech developers are doing just that.

The COVID pandemic accelerated the adoption of digital health tools in unexpected ways, including some of the digital health applications I've just described. Now, healthcare's stakeholders are working together as never before, eager to reap the benefits of what has become an unprecedented wave of innovation. Government policymakers and institutions are relaxing legal provisions and reimbursement requirements in ways that are benefiting health payers and providers alike. CMS has even developed new methods for reimbursing. All of these positive market indicators have sent an encouraging signal to employers and health insurers to keep reaching for the leading edge of health-tech development. I hope you'll be one of them!

ON A PERSONAL NOTE

I'm living proof that thoughts and beliefs are powerful when translated into action. Taking charge of your thought-life is going to be key to your success. Every person's life and business journey are characterized by ups and downs, sometimes on a daily basis. In the morning, your company (or your family) may be doing well and celebrate a big win—then suffer an unexpected setback by the afternoon. *Learning to ride out these ups and downs and understand why they've happened is an essential business asset.* Such understanding enables a deepening of resolve and the course corrections needed to drive the success of any venture. Still, my personal philosophy is that, in the end, what is meant to be will be. This pragmatic way of thinking fosters the bold business approach necessary in our current era of digital tech transformation.

Like everyone, I've experienced unexpected hardship and sorrow along with personal/professional joy. And I've found it is in the midst of the storm—including the striving, living, and learning—that meaning emerges and purpose is created. As a physician, my purpose is to help people. And I believe I can accomplish this more effectively with digital tech innovation and do it in a way that produces value for all stakeholders. Everyone in the healthcare and technology sectors can work to achieve that goal, and I invite them to join me in doing so.

Regardless of inherited IQ or our circumstances at birth, we can all practice business epigenetics, adding skills (reading, market analyses, public speaking) and traits (patience, humility, warmth) that will make us better at business and as human beings overall.

We're all going to need those skills and traits as the global environment continues to change. That's why I tell pioneers to prepare for the next iteration by becoming more curious, agile, open, and teachable. Change is the only factor that's constant, so while you're adapting, I encourage you to strive to be internally content, even if you're not feeling all that successful externally. In other words, it's important to cultivate the behaviors, traits, character, and skills that will best express your inner drive, audacity, power, and confidence—even when you feel as if you have none of those attributes yet.

Like a pro-surfer catching the ultimate wave, you can fearlessly "shoot the curl" of change by celebrating every victory—big or little. Ultimately, you'll achieve the most by living your life courageously, enjoying the freedom, empowerment, and satisfaction that it brings. Only *you* can determine what you really want and how you'll define your well-being, successes, learning, career, family, and values. We're in uncharted technological waters, making it impossible to predict every outcome. But the power of choice is still yours, and how you opt to respond to situations and people will determine your future. I wish you all the luck in the world in your healthcare journey, wherever this book finds you.

GLOSSARY

TERM	DEFINITION
Administrative Cost	Expenses associated with vendor fees, FTE support, marketing, etc.
Earned Premium	Any fee or other contribution associated paid by policy-holder in order to receive coverage from a health payer
Fully Insured	Large group, small group, and individual funding arrangement, which requires employers/members to pay a premium in exchange for a payer to assume the responsibility and related financial risk for paying healthcare expenses
Medical Billing Unit	Claim is categorized as a medical expense and is expensed against plan premium (e.g. Large Group and Small Group plans); require appropriate classification validation
Medical Claims	Healthcare benefits or clinical services
Medical Loss Ration (MLR)	A basic financial measurement used in the Affordable Care Act to encourage health plans to provide value to enrollees
Quality Improvement Expenditures	Benefit expenses to enhance the quality of insurance products
Self-Insured (also known as Administrative Services Only (ASO))	A funding arrangement in which employers can choose services that are the most appropriate for them and their employees while actively participating in the management of their health benefit plan; in this type of arrangement, employers are charged an administration fee and the employer group is responsible for payment of all claims
Stop Loss Coverage (also known as excess insurance)	A product that provides protection against catastrophic or unpredictable losses; often purchased by employers with a self-insured/ASO funding arrangement to manage liability arising form the plans; under a stop loss policy, the payer becomes liable for losses that exceed the deductible
Total Cost of Care	Total cost of a population and what it costs to care for them medically

Printed in the USA
CPSIA information can be obtained
at www.ICGtesting.com
JSHW021936110524
62941JS00001B/1

9 781642 258011